GREENWICH
MILLENNIUM

GREENWICH MILLENNIUM

The 2000-year Story of Greenwich

Clive Aslet

Fourth Estate • London

This paperback edition published in 1999
First published in Great Britain in 1999 by
Fourth Estate Limited
6 Salem Road
London W2 4BU
www.4thestate.co.uk

Copyright © Clive Aslet 1999

1 3 5 7 9 10 8 6 4 2

The right of Clive Aslet to be identified as the author of this work has been
asserted by him in accordance with the Copyright, Designs and Patents Act 1988.

A catalogue record for this book is available from the British Library.

ISBN 1-84115-234-X

Picture research by Juliet Brightmore
Designed by Robert Updegraff
Colour separations by ArtiColor, Verona
Printed in Great Britain by Bath Press

Title page **The Greenwich waterfront in 1835. The majestic hospital
rises serenely above the bustling wharves and river life.**

CONTENTS

Prologue   *9*

A Dead Stick Bursts into Leaf   19

La Maison de Grenevwyc   32

If You Are the Dauphin of France, I Wish to Kiss You   43

Love and Kindness Increase Daily between Them   61

I Have Never Lived So Merrily as I Have Done
This Plague-Time   89

Last Light on the Wave of Time   118

Sir John Vanbrugh Plays at Castles   139

As Much Honour and Delight as This World
Can Give   150

Arcadian Life among the Cockneys   176

All Honour to the Enderbys   187

The World Sets its Watch   215

The Millennium Comes in with a Roar   224

Further Reading   235
Principal Sources   236
Illustration Sources and Credits   241
Index   242

To Johnny

I would like to thank the following for their help in making this book: Pieter van der Merwe, an historian as well as resident of Greenwich, who not only provided many insights but also read the manuscript; Julian Bowsher and other archaeologists in the Museum of London for steering me through Greenwich's early history; the incomparable Lucy Pelz and Virginia Forrester, for additional research; Richard Ormond, director of the National Maritime Museum; and antiquarian, restaurateur and Greenwich resident, Dick Moy. Julian Watson and the staff of the Greenwich Local History Library have gone beyond the call of duty, as has Ralph Hyde, Keeper of Prints and Maps at the Guildhall Library. Mr Watson also read the manuscript. Juliet Brightmore's triumph in picture research speaks for itself. I owe a special debt to my editor Clive Priddle because he had the original idea for this book. But any errors in it are entirely my own.

Prologue

Each new day that dawns upon the world officially starts at Greenwich. Greenwich lies a few miles to the south-east of London. For centuries there was a royal palace here, and in its grounds the Royal Observatory was established in 1675. One of the principal functions of the early Astronomers Royal was to tabulate the apparent movement of the stars and planets across the night sky. Their charts were used by seamen to calculate longitude. Since the observations were made at Greenwich, they assumed Greenwich to lie on the prime meridian, or zero longitude. There were other charts and other prime meridians, but, courtesy of the British Empire, the Greenwich data came to be the most commonly used. As a result, from 1874 Greenwich has been internationally accepted as the point where zero longitude is drawn. The conference at which this was agreed also adopted zero longitude as the legally recognised date line for the world. By the end of the century, most nations accepted the time calculated from Greenwich as being the standard. France stubbornly held out. But even there, the patriotic deputies to the Assemblée Nationale managed, in 1896, to come up with the formula of Paris Mean Time diminished by nine minutes and twenty-one seconds – Greenwich time by another name. New methods of measuring time – even more precise than before – caused Universal Time to supersede Greenwich Mean Time in the 1970s. But the difference between Universal Time and Greenwich time is less than a second.

So there is every reason to celebrate the birth of the third millennium AD at Greenwich. The British government recognised this when they designated an area of derelict industrial land on what had once been Greenwich Marsh as the site of the Millennium Dome. It lies at one end of a loop made by the river Thames, meandering towards the sea. Take the riverside walk westwards, through a landscape of wharves and warehouses that seems to have nothing to do with the metropolitan London of which it is part, and you will come to the historic centre of Greenwich. This is the other end of the loop, where the river turns towards the City of London. With its royal palace – the open land behind it is still a royal park – the people of Greenwich inevitably found the events of national history entering forcibly into their own lives. They would have been particularly conscious of Britain's fortunes in war. To either side of them lay the dockyards of Woolwich and Deptford, while a hospital for wounded seamen stood in their midst. Kings, queens, courtiers, admirals, statesmen, regicides, successful merchants, industrialists and famous politicians – the inhabitants of Greenwich had the opportunity to view many national figures at close quarters. But they would also have seen squalor and want in the mean alleys that formed such a contrast to the grandeur of the palace, the public architecture and the houses of the rich. They would have witnessed both the elegant pastimes of the aristocracy and the demotic boisterousness of hoi polloi taking their holiday fun in Greenwich Park. Rebels, such as Jack Cade's rabble and the followers of the Peasants' Revolt, have assembled on the plateau of windswept land above the Park, known as Blackheath. So have Henry VIII's sea captains and George III's soldiery. But the Park is probably more familiar with golf balls than with musket balls – golf being one of the many peaceable activities for which this open space has served. The Royal Blackheath Golf Club is thought to be the oldest outside Scotland. This book traces the events and contrasts of the past millennium, experienced by the locality chosen to welcome the next one.

The peninsula where the Dome stands has its own history, first as low-lying farmland wrested from the tides, then as one of the busy, clamorous places that brought such wealth to Britain in the nineteenth and early twentieth centuries. The line of zero longitude crosses it, nicking the rim of the Dome. A building named after the millennium ought to be a wonder, and the Dome does not disappoint. It has been built on an extraordinary scale, using novel techniques and in record time. There was controversy at its inception – of course there was. But when the fireworks of New Year's Day, 2000, lit up the 100-metre tall masts, it seemed magically to dissolve. Controversy, it should be noted, is nothing new in Greenwich. The first astronomer royal, John Flamsteed, fell out with all the great scientists of his time, including Isaac Newton, and the Royal Naval Hospital, which now looks so magnificent, tottered from one financial crisis to another during the half-century that it took to build.

Visitors to the Dome are invited to experience a collage of sensations, exploring the universe of which mankind is part. The message is, according to the chief executive of the New Millennium Experience Company, Jenny Page: 'Be curious about the world.' There are fifteen themes, or zones, to engage the visitor's imagination. These have been designed to stimulate minds about some of the most vital strands of modern and future life. All of them are enriched by the context within which the Dome is located. For Greenwich and its immediate environs can be read as an essay on those very themes that are displayed so compellingly in the Millennium Experience.

Inside the Dome, the zone called Self-Portrait evokes the common heritage which binds the British people together. Outside the Dome, Greenwich as a whole is almost an emblem of national identity. For centuries, every great national event found its echo in Greenwich. It was in Greenwich Palace, or Placentia, that Henry VIII and Elizabeth I were born. Greenwich is remarkable for the thriving spirit that has attracted not just royalty, but commoners, merchants, entrepreneurs, and traders throughout its history. These industrious inhabitants have left a strong legacy, not just in terms of business. They have, in turn, established an extraordinary number of charities. The almshouses called Queen Elizabeth's College, founded in 1575, were the first public charity to have been established since the Reformation. (They were rebuilt in 1819 and now stand opposite the railway station.) After them came Trinity Hospital, the Grey Coat School, the Free Grammar School, the Green Coat School and the Blue Coat School, as well as the Royal Naval Hospital with its associated orphanage and school. There cannot be many locations in Britain where so much charitable endeavour has been concentrated in one place.

The Dome's Journey zone looks to the future of travel. Historically, the theme of the Journey could hardly be more closely reflected in Greenwich, with its ancient traditions of seafaring and shipbuilding. Even the railway has the distinction of being both the first to be built in London and the first suburban railway in the world. Ironically, the one form of transport to which Greenwich has never comfortably adapted itself is that epitomised by the Journey zone's sponsor, the Ford motor company; there would be greater sympathy, I suspect, with the Dome's policy of being a car-free destination. On the other hand, the Greenwich men who joined ships such as Sir Francis Drake's *Pelican* (renamed the *Golden Hind*) as they left Deptford, or who later penetrated the icebergs of the South Atlantic in pursuit of whales, would have relished the zone of Home Planet, with its theme of 'the most incredible sights, places and natural phenomena you have ever seen'. The crews of that adopted Greenwich fixture the *Cutty Sark*, bringing back tea from China and wool from Australia, must have seen some sights too. It is in the nature of Greenwich to be outward-looking: a certain cosmopolitanism is only to be expected of somewhere that, for over four hundred years, was the property of a Flemish abbey. Ships bring sailors, and sailors sometimes stay.

The zone called Shared Ground is about Britain's capacity to absorb, and thrive from, different cultures. Throughout history, people of all faiths and origins have rubbed along happily at Greenwich. Looking at nineteenth-century prints of the Royal Hospital, it is striking to see that black sailors sometimes qualified to become pensioners, without any prejudice against them being recorded. As early as 1759, Briton Hamilton had been an inmate there, dictating his autobiography – the first of a black man in Britain – because he could not read. Greenwich parish records show that there had been black servants attached to families around Greenwich and Blackheath since the seventeenth century. When those families were West Indian planters, the servants were sometimes slaves. Ambrose Crowley, the iron founder who gave his name to Crowley House, a mansion that stood on the site of the present power station, had a regrettable line in the supply of manacles, ankle irons and collars to slaving vessels. But the parish registers show that there were also a number of independent black people living in eighteenth-century Greenwich, neither slaves nor in service. Twenty-seven black people were baptised between 1754 and 1813. And both the eighteenth century's most famous black men, Ignatius Sancho and Olaudah Equiano, had a connection with Greenwich. Sancho, whose posthumously published *Letters* became a bestseller, acquired his first taste of society at Montagu House, on Blackheath, as butler to the Duke of Montagu. The Montagus educated him, and he became a poet, playwright and composer. To Equiano, sold into slavery for a few handfuls of cowrie shells, Greenwich was the nearest thing to home in a life without parents or personal security.

As for the Money zone, just remember the furious industrial activity that took place on Greenwich Marsh in the nineteenth century: evidence enough that Greenwich people have been as keen on turning a profit as anyone. Across the river from Greenwich Park the landscape is dominated by Canary Wharf, so tall that it has to be topped by a flashing light. The endless blink of that light can be taken as a metaphor for the worlds of commerce that this building serves: they never stop. Similarly the Work zone: Greenwich tradesmen – knife grinders, window menders, chimney sweeps – formed the subject of a photographic dossier compiled in 1885, and no more than a glance is needed to realise that they knew all about work. Look at them if you want to remember how far work has changed (or sometimes not changed) over the last century and a half.

I am not sure, though, that Play is not even more pertinent to Greenwich. Henry VIII would have thought so. Play was very much his idea of Placentia, as the palace built by his father was then known; it was at Greenwich that he built the first permanent tiltyard for his favourite sport of jousting. Later, from the age of Samuel Pepys, Greenwich and its park became a place of resort and recreation for Londoners, in search of green space and tranquillity. Twice a year it accommodated the less than tranquil Greenwich Fair, until this demotic, indecorous event was banned by the Victorians. In the Regency period, Princess Caroline, living riotously at Blackheath after her separation from the future George IV, may have taken Play rather too far. George III came to think so, though the people of Greenwich remained loyal to her throughout the attacks and trial for adultery that she suffered.

The Learning and Mind zones have their counterpart in the scientific tradition at Greenwich. Specifically, this was focused on the Royal Observatory, though it is also striking how many of the inventive, full-bottom-wigged gentlemen who made up the Royal Society lived in the area. The National Maritime Museum, which now operates the old Royal Observatory, is itself a repository of learning, not only in the galleries that are visited by the public but also in its vast library of nautical records. Now the buildings of the Royal Naval Hospital, more recently the Royal Naval College, are home to the University of Greenwich.

Visitors to the Talk zone, sponsored by British Telecom, may care to remember that the first transatlantic cable was manufactured only a few hundred yards from where they are standing, at the works of William Kuper and Company at East Greenwich.

The Living Island zone emphasises the importance of maintaining a healthy environment. That principle is admirably demonstrated by Greenwich, part of whose appeal has always been its 'salubrious air'. Or, as Edward Hasted put it in his *History of Kent*, 1778: 'The dryness and salubrity of the soil, the convenience of the park, the general pleasantness of the adjoining country, and its near neighbourhood to the metropolis, contribute to make it a most desirable residence for people of fashion.' The people of fashion ganged up to strike a blow for the environment – remarkable, given the laissez-faire spirit of the times – when they prevented the railway pushing eastwards across the Park. This blighted the prospects of development in East Greenwich, which might otherwise have become docks. (Where then should we have built the Millennium Dome?) But it showed that, even in the most rampant phase of Victorian capitalism, the claims of the environment could sometimes take priority over commercial gain.

Greenwich and its neighbour Blackheath have always been regarded as civilised places to live, partly because of their association with the zone of Rest. In fact, the area around Greenwich has always made a speciality of its restorative features. As early as the Tudor period, City merchants built country houses here. In the eighteenth century, the fashion was for villas: elegant residences, surrounded by attractive grounds, that were convenient for London. The insurance underwriter John Julius Angerstein, whose collection would form the nucleus of the National Gallery, built Woodlands, now the local history library. The open land of Blackheath, when not being used to muster troops, was used for the promotion of Rest, through the host of sporting activities that took place there.

The Dome celebrates the workings of the body in the Body zone. By far the most impressive homage to the body in Greenwich was when Nelson's body was brought there for his lying in state after the Battle of Trafalgar. It was displayed in the Painted Hall of the Naval Hospital to unprecedented public mourning. Bodies have been put on show in Greenwich for far less noble purposes. Hanged pirates' remains were left dangling from the gibbet on Execution Dock – only a stone's throw from the Dome – until three tides had washed over them. A portion of Jack Cade's corpse was displayed on Blackheath after the rebel had been hanged, drawn and quartered.

More cheerfully, Greenwich has sustained the body with its fine food, especially fish. In the nineteenth century entire Cabinets of politicians, both Liberal and Conservative, would descend on the Trafalgar and the Ship taverns to consume whitebait suppers.

Tribute to the spiritual dimension of the millennium – a landmark of the Christian calendar – is paid by the zone devoted to Faith. The story of Greenwich contains some striking examples of the workings of Faith. At the very beginning of the previous millennium, Greenwich acquired its own saint – St Alfege – an archbishop of Canterbury who was martyred by the Vikings. The Viking longships were moored in the elbow of the Thames where Greenwich now stands. They stayed there the whole winter, and poor Alfege was dragged to the Viking encampment after the sack of Canterbury. His death is supposed to have taken place in the grounds of the parish church. In commemoration, the present church, built by Hawksmoor after the collapse of its medieval precursor, is dedicated to him. Visitors to the Faith zone can reflect on what connection, if any, might exist between the Greenwich saint and the Greenwich temple, the remains of which, dating from around AD 100, have been revealed on the brow of a hill in Greenwich Park. They should also spare a thought for the Observant friars who lived in the monastery next to the Palace. On an electric occasion in 1532, one of them, William Peto, preached an Easter sermon before Henry VIII on the evils of divorce, threatening Britain with excommunication. Peto escaped with his life. The other friars were arrested when they refused to take an oath of allegiance and thirty of them died horribly in prison.

Altogether, the Millennium Experience is about where we have come from, where we are and where we are going. It was no accident that Greenwich, synonymous with time, was chosen as its location. The new millennium literally starts here. With its glorious architecture, Greenwich has been a place of famous landmarks since at least the seventeenth century. The arrival of the Dome has added another to the tally. But the relationship between the Dome and the Borough within which it has arisen is more than geographical. The immense themes that have been brought so inspiringly to life beneath the great curving trusses of the Dome are graphically embodied, on a human scale, in the real-life story of Greenwich.

A DEAD STICK
BURSTS INTO LEAF

I T IS APPROPRIATE, given that the millennium celebrations
begins at Greenwich, that its history should start with the
martyrdom of a Christian saint. St Alfege may not be the
most famous in the canon, but he is at least Greenwich's own.
The parish church is the only one in Britain to be dedicated to
him. His death took place at the dawn of the second millennium
after Christ.

Things had happened before that at Greenwich, of course. But
nothing was written down about any habitation that existed
before the end of the first millennium, and the evidence of archae-
ology is inconclusive. It would not be surprising if prehistoric or
Celtic people had chosen to settle here, since the site, at the point
where a tributary of the Thames joins the main river, would have
looked inviting. Before the Thames was confined within its
Victorian embankments, it would have seemed like a wide band of
fraying cloth, much broader and shallower than the present river,
constantly overflowing its poorly defined banks, and encumbered
by dozens of little islands. To either side would have been mudflats, reedbeds and marshes. Behind the marshes rose clumps of
trees, oaks, some of them centuries old. Wading birds with long
beaks – spoonbills, herons, cranes – fished along the mudflats.
They were joined by otters and water voles, while beavers busied
themselves damming streams. Brown bears, wolves, elk, wild boar,

19

badgers and red deer roamed among the trees and beside the water. Apart from the cries of the animals and birds, it would, for the most part, have been silent.

The river itself provided a means by which journeys could be made. So did the little brook that joined it, called the Ravensbourne. Travelling any distance by land was practically impossible in an age of few roads. From the river also came fish. The birds that fed along the reedbeds provided another source of food. The fur of the beavers, otters and other creatures could be made into clothes. Walls could be made by weaving together the osiers that grew by the river and covering them with mud. Reeds could be worked into baskets. Even the grasses from the marsh might be plaited together to make cups. Near the river, the land rises steeply to the bluff where the old Royal Observatory was to be built, and beyond it is the plateau of Blackheath. Not much more than gorse would have grown on the wretched, waterless soil of the heath itself. But around and about there were woods, which had an obvious usefulness.

One man, thousands of years ago, had been working in the woods, hacking at a tree with a piece of sharpened stone. It was a milky grey stone, oval in section, ground and polished at the edge. Somehow it became lost in the undergrowth; perhaps he dropped it, or perhaps it flew out of his hand. It must have been a precious possession, to someone who had very few possessions of any kind, but he did not manage to recover it. There it lay, beside the Thames, until it was discovered in the twentieth century and put into the Museum of London. (Or so I like to think. Less romantically, it may just as well have been carried there from somewhere else by the tide.)

To the west of Greenwich, the Romans came and established a port out of what had previously been a scattering of homesteads, at a point where the river, more than usually broad, looked almost like a lake flowing around an archipelago of little islands. They called this port Londinium. Immediately east of Greenwich there was already a settlement of huts, huddling behind the earthworks that would protect them from marauders, at Charlton; most evidence of it was destroyed when sand was dug from the area in the eighteenth and nineteenth centuries. The Celts who lived there farmed, made pots and worked iron. The Greenwich Borough Museum now contains some of the humble debris of their lives, a rather sad assemblage of flint flakes, querns, clay-loom weights, two brooches, bone pins, fragments of coarse pottery, two coins bearing the head of Emperor Claudius, on whose order an army of forty thousand men invaded Britain in AD 43 – not much to leave behind from three centuries of continuous occupation. There are one or two farmsteads that we know about from the domestic debris that has been found, but they may not have been permanent dwellings. No doubt other such habitations existed, surrounded by fields and linked to each other by paths. If there was one at Greenwich, any trace of it has been lost as a result of the centuries of building work that have taken place there.

The Romans built the first identifiable roads. One of them was Watling Street, connecting the ports of Rochester and Dover with London. This road seems to have come over the brow of Shooter's Hill, clipped the corner of what became the royal park and kissed the Thames at Greenwich, before marching onwards, straight as could be, to the ford at Westminster. At the point when Watling Street reached the river at Greenwich, there may have been a dock or even a ferry; certainly there was a ferry here in later centuries. (It is marked as a horse ferry on John Rocque's map of 1746, showing that it was intended for carts as well as people. It must have been part of a fairly important route running south from Old Ford, through the Isle of Dogs.) Traces of what could have been Watling Street were uncovered during the digging of a gas main in the 1960s.

Just off Watling Street, in what is now Greenwich Park, stood a temple. People may have thought that spirits lived in the woods here. The temple stood all alone on the hill. At the beginning of this century, when its mosaic pavement was discovered, archaeologists thought it was a villa; they even imagined that they had discovered the site of a lost settlement, known from descriptions of the Roman roads as Noviomagus. More recent investigations suggest the villa theory to be false. The building was probably raised in this remote area to celebrate some cult. The men and women visiting it left their tribute in the form of hundreds of Roman coins that have since been unearthed. The earliest of these dates from about AD 70.

There was a statue in the temple: an arm holding drapery is all that has been found of it. Unfortunately the inscriptions on the fragments of stone that have been discovered are mostly illegible. The letters C V L A P, or what appear to be such, might come from Aesculapius, the Roman god of medicine. If so, it records the origin of an association with health-giving properties that survived into the seventeenth century, when Queen Anne of Denmark took the waters here. Perhaps other buildings were grouped around the temple to service it. One would think so from the quantity of animal bones and mollusc shells, as well as rough pottery and other objects, that have been excavated.

When, towards the end of the fourth century AD, Rome began to lose its grip on the world, places like London were vulnerable to the general administrative collapse. So bustling in the second century, so cosmopolitan in its tastes, London began to decline as a port, and then as a city. When the Emperor pulled out his troops from England, it suffered further. Eventually, by the middle of the fifth century, the inhabitants abandoned it. There was no one from London to make the pilgrimage to the shrine at Greenwich. Watling Street grew over with weeds.

What used to be called the Dark Ages are, for Greenwich, precisely that. There is little to illuminate whatever harsh existence was played out beside this curve of the Thames. Next to nothing, then, about life; but a little more is known of its concomitant, death. On the west side of Greenwich Park a series of hummocks on the ground are the remains of Saxon burial mounds, the earliest of which dates from the seventh century. The men were put into the ground with their shields and spears. Some of these weapons were discovered when an antiquarian called the Reverend James Douglas excavated eighteen of these barrows in the late eighteenth century. Douglas also found what he took to be the decayed traces of wooden coffins, though no human bones. There were fifty of the barrows in Douglas's time but we have no further evidence of the lives of the people who were buried in them. Clearly the group must have been related to a centre of some size. In Saxon place names the suffix 'wich' signifies port or market. Green Market – it has rather a modern ring.

The first glimmer of light in Greenwich's history comes in 964. In that year, King Edgar, who liked to call himself Emperor of Britain, granted the manor of Lewisham, including Greenwich, to foreign owners: St Peter's Abbey in Ghent. This provides the first written reference to Greenwich. The document mentions churchyards, cultivated land, crops, woods, meadows and pastures, giving the impression that it was already well settled. But the monks and their possessions must have been all too accessible to foreigners of another stamp. Since the late eighth century, long narrow boats, their square sails supplemented by oars – elegant vessels with their prows and ends turned up like Turkish slippers – had been snaking their way across the North Sea from Denmark, and up the estuaries and rivers of England. These were the Viking longships, full of salt-caked, ferocious raiders who seemed devoid of all pity for the shore people whose livings they plundered. They must have been a terrifying sight to anyone who observed them making their swift, silent way along even quite small rivers. Greenwich saw more than it would have liked of them. The loop in the river provided a good harbour, near to the riches of London, perhaps with a shingle beach onto which boats could be pulled up. By the end of the tenth century, the fleets, fifty long-ships at a time, were coming often, and sometimes staying over winter. The open land of Blackheath provided somewhere for the warriors to camp. In 1012 the Vikings came, anchored at Greenwich and did not leave for three years.

In the course of this campaign the Vikings besieged Canterbury. The town ran out of food after twenty days, and the archbishop, who was Alfege, sent messengers to remonstrate with them. It was no use. They set fire to the town, broke through the wall and, in the words of the eighteenth-century volume *Britannia Sancta, or the Lives of the Most Celebrated British, English, Scottish and Irish Saints*, 'made a terrible slaughter of all they met, without distinction of either sex or age'. Alfege, by this time immured within the cathedral with his monks, ventured out, begging them to spare the 'poor harmless people'. Their response was to seize him by the throat, bind his hands and beat him up, 'which, in imitation of his Redeemer, he suffered with wonderful meekness and silence'.

Alfege, it will be gathered, was a figure of extraordinary piety. Born into a noble family, he had turned his back on worldly pos-sessions by entering a monastery. Even this was not enough for him, and he became an anchorite at Bath. So many people came to consult him there that they founded a monastery. St Andrew supposedly appeared in a dream to St Dunstan, the Archbishop of Canterbury, recommending St Alfege to the see of Winchester, following the death of its bishop: 'thus was he forced out of his solitude.' When St Dunstan himself died, Alfege succeeded him. En route to Rome to receive his pall from the Pope, he was attacked by brigands – whereupon the town that the ruffians came from was consumed with flames until they relented, imploring Alfege to persuade God to stop burning their homes. The miserable ravaging of England by the Danes was, to this holy man, merely another opportunity to exercise his charity, 'as well in relieving and redeeming the English, whom these barbarous invaders had ruined or enslaved; as in preaching the word of life to the Danes, a great number of whom he converted to the faith of Christ'.

His preaching did not, however, make much of an impression on the men who had captured Alfege at Canterbury. They cared nothing for his piety and culture. They dragged him to Greenwich, locked him up in a damp cell infested with frogs and put his feet into irons. They began to feel differently after his intervention with God cured them of the 'violent torments in their bowels' that had beset them; but their offer to release him for a ransom of three thousand marks was spurned. His parishioners were too destitute to raise it. It caused the Vikings to treat him more cruelly than ever.

There was an attempt at rescuing him. A man appeared at the cell door one night, holding a flaming torch and quoting Scripture. Alfege followed him, hoping to escape over the streams and ditches of the marsh. The captors quickly realised he was gone and set off in pursuit. It was an unequal contest. Alfege stumbled

Greenwich and Blackheath, from the Survey of London published by
John Rocque in 1746. At this date Greenwich and Blackheath were
surrounded by country houses, such as Sir Gregory Page's Wricklemarsh
estate, shown south-east of the park.

along on feet that had been damaged by the manacles, and was unable to keep up. Finally he fell into a bog. The Danes seized him once again. They told him that

> either he must furnish them with the gold they demanded, or must die. He replied, that he had no other gold to bestow, but the gold of true wisdom, consisting in the knowledge and worship of the true and living God, which he was willing to impart to them: but if they continued obstinately to refuse this, he told them they would one day fare worse than Sodom; and that their Empire should not be long lived in England.

It was not the answer they wanted. They now had a grand prisoner who was useless to them. They held a council in their campaign hall, made of a great leather-sided tent; and afterwards they got to feasting. As the evening degenerated, they began hurling abuse and bits of food at Alfege. All of this he suffered in his holy way, quoting Scripture. This, however, only provoked the Danes to throw bones at him. Eventually an ox head was hurled in his direction, knocking him to the ground. One Dane, whom Alfege had baptised only the previous day, then split open his skull with an axe. By tradition, the murder is supposed to have taken place on the site of the parish church.

The slaughter of an archbishop was an outrage, even by the brutal standards of the Danes. Apparently it so distressed Thurkill, commander of the Danes at Greenwich, who was an unwilling witness at the scene, that he changed sides, offering his services – and his forty-five ships – to the English King Ethelred. The ships remained at Greenwich, and there must have been much local rejoicing when it was discovered that Sweyn, the Danish leader, had sailed to attack the Humber instead of the Thames. But he marched southwards, conquering all. Soon Ethelred had fled to the Isle of Wight, and thence to Normandy, aboard one of Thurkill's ships. And Greenwich continued as the centre of the Danish occupations. It took piles of Danegeld to persuade them to go.

It was not long before relics of martyred Alfege were believed to have caused miracles. Probably he became credited with powers that were formerly the property of quite other kinds of deity. It was said that when a dead stick was sprinkled with his blood and fixed in the ground, it burst into leaf the next morning.

In the Tudor period, there was an image of 'Saint Alphey' in the choir of the parish church, with another of the Virgin Mary. One parishioner left 6s 8d to put a light before it in 1509, and the vicar Edmond Russell wished to be buried in front of it in 1486. Like many medieval structures, the church of St Alfege was built more on faith than engineering science. The digging of graves in the nave of the church, too near the pillars, had weakened such foundations as it possessed, and they were probably not much good anyway. On a stormy November night in 1710 one of the pillars of the nave gave way and a large part of the roof came crashing down. Except for the tower at the west, the old fabric was deemed too rotten to repair, and whatever had not collapsed was demolished.

Greenwich now had no church, and no money to build another one. A petition was sent to Parliament, painting the destitution of the parish in lurid colours. It was a good moment to present it. Only the previous month the Tories had come into government, and they prided themselves on being the Church of England party. The Greenwich petition persuaded Parliament not just to rebuild St Alfege's but to construct a total of fifty new churches throughout London. The architect of the new St

Bust of Nicholas Hawksmoor by Sir Henry Cheere.

Alfege's was Nicholas Hawksmoor, formerly assistant to Sir Christopher Wren.

Few parish churches in England can rival St Alfege's for the drama of its east portico – a composition on a giant scale, inspired by Alberti's fifteenth-century portico in Mantua. By this date, it was nothing new for an English church to be built in a classical style, as all kinds of religious buildings had been throughout Europe since the Renaissance. But the grand classical manner, so obviously intended to emulate the grandeur of ancient Rome, has a special, if ironic, appropriateness in a church dedicated to a saint whose miraculous powers may partly have been borrowed from the deities associated with the pagan Roman temple in the woods at Greenwich.

Lithograph of St Alfege's Church, Greenwich, viewed from Stockwell Street. The church was built by Nicholas Hawksmoor in 1711, with the steeple added by John James in 1730.

LA MAISON
DE GRENEVWYC

GREENWICH HAS ALWAYS been cosmopolitan. Its position on the Thames has made it the home of sailors and merchants, people who travelled far through their professional bond with the sea, foreigners who first touched English land at Greenwich, or thereabouts, and stayed there. The longest association in its history, in terms of ownership, has been with the Abbey of St Peter in Ghent. This began, as we have seen, as an outright gift, at a time when the common allegiance to Christendom was stronger than a sense of English nationhood. As England came to cohere as a state, the monarch – a succession of monarchs – managed to weaken the foreign abbot's hold on Greenwich, perfectly lawful though it was, until it fell from his grasp altogether. Being rather more than a bauble, it was picked up, put in the royal pocket, treasured and polished until it sparkled as one of the most splendid palaces and royal building sites in the land.

Far away in Ghent, the abbots suffered the unpopularity that is usually the lot of absentee landlords, and with reason. In the thirteenth century they, or their representatives, flouted the law of the land by inflicting an illegal toll of a penny-halfpenny on woolcarts that crossed the king's highway on the way to the quay. The local people, of course, hated these imposts, and whipped up all sorts of ill feeling towards the foreign monks. It was said that the large number of foreigners living in this strategic site on the Thames imperilled national security. This gave Edward III an excuse to take the abbey's lands into his own custody, supposedly as a defensive measure during the Hundred Years War against France. Around Christmas time, in the year 1366, two attendants, a pipe of salted beef, eight bacons and three barrels of beer set off for Flanders. With them went the then prior. He never came back.

Without a prior, the monks struggled on, disheartened and increasingly lax, until their possessions, along with those of other foreign monasteries, were confiscated by Henry V in 1414. The end for the monks had been a long time in coming. For Greenwich, it was a beginning.

There was by now a big house by the river at Greenwich: it is not known exactly when, or by whom, it was built, though in the twelfth century it was already being referred to as old. It stood roughly on the site of the palace that would later be built by the Tudors, and established this location by the strand of the Thames as somewhere to live. A description comes from the end of the fourteenth century, when the abbot of St Peter's, Ghent, realising that the Flemish presence at Greenwich was at its last gasp, dispatched an agent called Gille Delaporte to report on what could be salvaged from the decline. The answer put an end to any hope of reasserting Flemish rights, since the reply to every question of ownership came back like a litany: 'On dit que le Roy les a tous.' People say that the king owns everything. 'La maison de Grenevwyc' was found to be well maintained, with a gatehouse roofed with tiles towards the fields. The only person who lived there, however, was a one-eyed concierge.

By this time, Greenwich had become firmly established as a fishing village, supported by wharves, boatyards and other maritime businesses. Greenwich ships are mentioned in thirteenth-century records. The place was sufficiently developed to have a church and a market, and it had already acquired its reputation as somewhere that rich London people could reside in the equivalent of villas. The property transactions that took place in the four-teenth century contain references to gardens and meadows.

Soon the big house on the river at Greenwich also acquired a literary reputation. It would put Greenwich at the heart of Renaissance culture in England: a position it occupied for as long as that culture persisted. Geoffrey Chaucer may very well have lived at Greenwich, or somewhere near, between 1385 and 1399, since he served almost continuously as a commissioner of the peace for Kent in those years, and in 1390 was appointed to a royal commission (of walls and ditches) along the banks of the Thames between Greenwich and Woolwich. From Greenwich he could presumably have watched the pilgrims heading for Canterbury as they made their way across Blackheath. The one or two references he made to Greenwich by name are not very com-plimentary. Many a shrew lived there, he wrote – a view that may have been personal or topical, rather than a general reflection.

In the late 1420s the manor of Greenwich came into the posses-sion of Humphrey Duke of Gloucester, the youngest brother of the dead King, Henry V. Humphrey was then Protector and Defender of England, as the uncle of Henry VI, who was only a child. Earlier in his career, he had won sufficient popularity from the citizens of London to be called the Good Duke. The epithet appears to derive from the valour with which he fought the French, both during Henry V's campaigns there, and later on his own account, when he made a buccaneering raid on the Pas de Calais and Flanders. London merchants approved of fierceness in battle: anything to the detriment of their commercial rivals in France suited their cause. By the time he acquired Greenwich, however, Humphrey was not quite so much the Good Duke: in fact he was doing everything he could (not quite successfully) to rule England as a despot. His capacity for sexual indulgence was regarded as excessive, even in a prince.

For all that, Duke Humphrey was also, through the associations he formed, a fountain of learning and humanism in a country as yet unwatered by Renaissance thought. He was dedicated to the new learning and corresponded with the Italian scholars who were the leaders of intellectual life in Europe. 'In no other Englishman of the time do we find the same love of the ancient classics which characterised Gloucester,' commented K. H. Vickers in his biography of 1907. At Greenwich he assembled the greatest private library of his age. He rebuilt the house there, complete with a watchtower that stood on the site of the present Royal Observatory (under the name of Duke Humphrey's Tower, it remained a local landmark for centuries). The name he gave his house was the manor of Plesaunce, or Bella Court.

It must have been intended to celebrate beauty and the softer arts of life, so absent from the military and political worlds that he was accustomed to inhabit.

Unlike the Plesaunce itself, the creation of the Duke's library is well documented. In the age before printing, merely to possess a collection of books was a contribution to scholarship. It was not easy to assemble them, given the labours of copying. The difficulties were particularly severe in the case of foreign works. The fashion for Italian literature was so great throughout Europe that the copyists could not meet the demand. Foreign patrons like Humphrey had to rely on authorities such as the Italian humanist Aretinus to supply them with texts, and Renaissance scholars were hardly scrupulous in matters of business. They had a habit of selling their expertise to whichever prince offered them most. All of which makes the scale of Humphrey's bibliophilia more impressive.

The size of Humphrey's library can be imagined from the extent of his benefactions to the University of Oxford. It was Humphrey's gifts of books that rescued Oxford from obscurity. This was a time when there were almost no books at the University, and all the teaching of students was done orally. So when Humphrey gave 129 books in 1438, the University's capacity to investigate outside ideas was transformed. There followed a further 150 books over the next few years. 'Gifts of books in such numbers were unique in the history of the University, and continued to be so for some time to come,' comments Vickers. They go some way towards justifying the tag of Good Duke Humphrey, which in other respects seems so strange. John Capgrave, who produced his *Chronicle of England* under the patronage of the Duke, may have overdone it when he called Humphrey 'the most lettered prince in the world'. But his house at Greenwich must have seemed a beacon of modern thought, housing not only a splendid collection of books but, from time to time, the most glittering literary figures of which England could boast.

Humphrey's life ended in disaster. At court, he was leader of the war party against France; his weak-minded nephew Henry VI sided with those who wanted peace. The King went so far as to take a French girl, the fifteen-year-old Margaret of Anjou, as his bride. Humphrey's enemies succeeded in poisoning her mind against the Duke.

In 1447, an unsuspecting Humphrey set off for Bury St Edmunds, with what could be regarded as a relatively compact retinue of eighty horsemen, to attend the Parliament there. On his arrival he was arrested. It is quite likely that an unnatural death had been planned for him. In fact, the shock of the arrest seems to have brought on a stroke, which paralysed him and deprived him of speech. After a few days he died. The fate that could have been in store for him had he not done so was then visited upon his supporters. Five of the most prominent of them, including his natural

Humphrey Duke of Gloucester, reckless soldier, notorious libertine and flawed statesman, he was also an early patron of Renaissance learning, whose library, housed at Greenwich, formed the basis of the Bodleian in Oxford.

son Arthur, were tried by his enemy, Lord Suffolk, and sentenced to be hanged, drawn and quartered. The accusation was that they had been plotting with Humphrey against the King, during a seditious meeting at Greenwich. It is a reflection of the unpopularity of these events with the populace that, just as they stood at Tyburn with a rope around their necks, they received a reprieve.

As soon as Humphrey was dead, Greenwich and many of his other possessions passed to the young Queen. To make it truly hers, she set about a campaign of decoration. Robert Kettlewell was summoned from the royal palace at Eltham to become 'Clerk of the Quenyswerkys of the maner of Plesaunce'. Into a bay window went fourteen feet of new glass 'floushyd cum margaritis' (flushed or coloured with daisies), the daisy being the Queen's device, a play on her name. Daisies had decorated everything at Nancy when the wedding took place. The King's flower was the hawthorn bud, and that also appeared in the glass. There must have been flowers, too, in the garden, where the Queen had an arbour. The flowers in the glass were made by John Pond; John Pruddle provided more stained glass for the chapel.

For what appears to have been the first time in England, Margaret organised her palace around two wards, or courts, one for her own apartments and one for the King's: a pattern which was to become standard in great royal residences. Brought up in France, Margaret was familiar with luxury, and there is a suggestion of it in her adornment of Greenwich. Altogether Margaret's house beside the Thames must have made a pretty sight, with its hawthorn buds and daisies and gaily contrasting pink brick and white stone. But the image of comfort and domesticity which it offered was an illusion. Whatever the appointments of the interior, these were not comfortable times.

Those men who brought about Humphrey Duke of Gloucester's downfall did not have long to enjoy their own eminence. Three years after his death, the Earl of Suffolk, impeached by Parliament, was banished to France, but the ship taking him there was intercepted by the *Nicholas of the Tower*, the crew of which tried and beheaded him. They may well have known Humphrey since the ship had taken soldiers to France for Henry V's wars, and the master, Henry Robinson, was a Greenwich man. The discontents caused Jack Cade to lead an uprising of Kentish men and women, who, like Wat Tyler's rabble, assembled on Blackheath, next to Greenwich, and camped there for over a month. Cade himself may have been Irish. An adventurer and an impostor, he simply saw the insurrection as his chance for – who knows what? A few days of power, during which he could wear scarlet clothes, behead insubordinates and terrify the solid citizens of London. Many of his followers, though, were local people, quite a number from Greenwich and apparently respectable. A few of them had been personally associated with Humphrey and were out to avenge his death which everyone thought had been murder. More surprisingly, they were accompanied by one Richard Henham, a Greenwich carpenter who had lately supplied beds to the Queen at the Plesaunce, and his wife.

Blackheath, an open space only a few miles from London, was a natural rallying ground for the discontented. Its proximity to Greenwich, so imbued with the spirit of Duke Humphrey, must have redoubled its relevance as the place where forces opposed to the regime which had apparently done away with him should congregate. Jack Cade's rebellion, which culminated in the execution of the Earl of Suffolk's associate, Lord Saye and Sele, was followed by the predictable reprisals: Cade himself was hunted down and butchered, one of his quarters being exhibited on Blackheath. Today he is commemorated by Cade Road. The men living around Blackheath, including those at Greenwich, were forced to ask the King's pardon on their knees, naked except for their shirts. There is some reason to call Cade's rebellion the first armed conflict in the Wars of the Roses. Only two years later, in 1452, another force assembled on Blackheath, composed of supporters of Richard, Duke of York; on this occasion the King backed down before the confrontation came to a head.

Once those wars had begun, it became too unsafe for Margaret of Anjou to linger at Greenwich, in this hostile neighbourhood, so she decamped for places of more solid Lancastrian support, such as the Midlands. The young Duke of York, his father having died fighting the Lancastrians at the Battle of Wakefield, entered London in 1461 and was crowned Edward IV. After a progress around England, he came to Greenwich to hunt in Duke Humphrey's park. He was six foot four tall and the epitome of chivalry. It is difficult to think that he did not marry for love. Certainly his choice of a wife, in 1464, otherwise seems eccentric, and she was famous for her black-

A condemned traitor was hung, drawn and quartered (as in this sixteenth-century engraving). One quarter of Jack Cade, the adventurer who led an insurrection in 1450, was exhibited on Blackheath, where his followers had camped.

haired beauty. She was Elizabeth Woodville (or Widville), from the manor of Lee, just on the other side of Blackheath from Greenwich. Soon after Edward IV's marriage to Elizabeth Woodville, he granted her 'the lordship and manor of Plesaunce, otherwise called Grenewiche, with the Tower of Grenewiche and the parks there'.

Edward IV was fully possessed of the Renaissance idea of magnificence, whereby it was not enough for a great man simply to be a great man – he had to show himself one through the splendour of his possessions, the prodigality of his gifts and the display of his effulgent self to his people.

So Edward IV glowed with this charisma of riches, while the more simple tastes of Henry VI seemed niggardly. Ostentation was all. It was a principle that prevailed in different forms until the death of Queen Elizabeth 140 years later. During that time Greenwich would blaze like gold.

Paradoxically, though, Edward IV's own special contribution was to establish a house of Observant Friars just next to the palace, on a piece of land 'where the game of ball used to be played'. They were a branch of the Franciscan order and lived according to a strict rule of poverty. By contrast, the King himself developed a reputation for 'boon-companionship, vanities, debaucheries, extravagance and sensual enjoyments', as a contemporary put it. This corpulent man died suddenly, at the age of forty, in 1483.

It was now all over for the Woodvilles. Many of Elizabeth's kinsmen were put to death, as were the little Princes in the Tower who were her sons. She herself survived the two years of Richard III's reign, and was assigned a pension by Henry Tudor when he came to the throne as Henry VII in 1485. Henry cemented the reconciliation between the Lancastrians and the Yorkists by marrying her daughter, Elizabeth of York. But he kept Greenwich for himself. Henry VII loved Greenwich.

IF YOU ARE THE DAUPHIN OF FRANCE, I WISH TO KISS YOU

ENRY VII EXPRESSED HIS LOVE for the Plesaunce, which he renamed Placentia, by demolishing most of it. But he built it up again into a new palace, bigger and more modern and far more splendid than the old.

It took some time for Henry VII to show that he was a king who would build. The first decade of his reign was spent consolidating his position; to embark on lengthy campaigns of construction cannot have seemed a priority until his own survival on the throne looked more certain. Blackheath was again the scene of insurrection when a great body of Cornishmen occupied it in 1497. It did not take much to defeat them, and carpenters from Placentia who had been building the 'Queen's barn' downed tools to watch the battle. Later, the Protestant martyr Hugh Latimer remembered helping his father buckle on his armour 'when he went unto Blackheath field'. (He mentioned it in a sermon preached before Edward VI.) There was a terrible slaughter, after which the dead were buried in heaps.

Another obstacle to building was Henry VII's initial shortage of money: fighting had emptied the royal coffers. But from the mid-1490s until his death in 1509 Henry VII spent £29,000 on his principal houses and even more on works of piety, such as the completion of King's College Chapel, Cambridge, and his own memorial chapel at Westminster. Foremost among the palaces were that which he renamed Richmond (formerly Sheen: he had been Duke of Richmond before taking the crown) and Placentia. It was a sign of the affection in which all the Tudors would hold Greenwich, where the future Henry VIII, Queen Mary and Queen Elizabeth were born.

Rich or poor, Henry VII came to the throne determined to celebrate. Magnificence was a weapon in his political armoury. A further incentive came from the many years of privation he had suffered before coming to the throne. So stupendous pomp accompanied his coronation, his wedding and such occasions as the creation of the little Prince Harry as Duke of York. He would give feasts for hundreds of people at a time. He loved books and music, but he also loved hunting. For that reason he preferred a country life, surrounded by fine horses, greyhounds and hawks. Greenwich must have satisfied this side of his nature, for it was in a completely rural location; yet it was close enough to London for the King, necessarily suspicious, to know everything that happened in his capital.

Richmond Palace had some of the fairy-tale quality associated with contemporary French architecture; with its little forest of bell-shaped domes, it suggested an enchanted castle – perfect and symmetrical. Greenwich was an altogether different proposition. There was no attempt to make it look like a fortress; this in itself was a novelty after so many years of civil war. It had no moat. Nor was it remotely symmetrical. From the chapel that stood at the eastern end of the site a long irregular façade unfolded westwards along the river, in a succession of projecting bays, buttresses and gables. Most of this range was two storeys tall, but towards the west end stood a squarish tower or donjon of five storeys. The donjon was a medieval survival.

The King's rooms overlooked the river; other accommodation was arranged round a series of courtyards. Apparently only a fireplace and one wall from the old Plesaunce were incorporated into Henry's new structure: probably the timber of which much of the previous house had been constructed had decayed. But the foundations would seem to have been reused, since archaeologists have discovered that the outline of the previous building was preserved within the new. The master mason Robert Vertue and his men carried out most of the work between 1500 and 1504, at a cost of £900. In 1504 Henry VII kept Christmas at Greenwich with the Marquis of Dorset and several other great figures. For the remaining few years of his reign, Greenwich frequently became the setting for the great religious festivals, such as Christmas, with all their associated junketing.

But Henry's heart was no longer in these celebrations. By the time Greenwich was finished, the gloom and parsimony for which Henry's character tends to be remembered had closed in. His earlier high spirits and love of display had evaporated. Two of his sons, including the eldest, Arthur, had died. Then his Queen, Elizabeth of York, died in childbirth in 1503. The King who came to occupy Greenwich for the first time the next year had lost much of his vitality. Although still in his forties, his hair had thinned, those few teeth that he had were black, his skin had turned sallow. It was too late for Placentia to provide the backdrop to spectacular shows of gaiety and revelling. It was left to his glamorous young son, Henry VIII, to fill the palace with people, vigour, courtship, colour, feasting, gorgeous clothes, enticing women and swaggering men.

* * *

When Henry VIII became King in 1509, he was seventeen, extremely handsome, so strong and brave that he often challenged all comers to fight him; he spoke French and Latin, understood Italian, composed music as well as played it on various instruments, sang tunefully and balanced his love of luxury with reading and frequent religious devotions. He was modern, thoughtful and sophisticated, though susceptible to the romance of the past. Magnificence was at the heart of his aesthetic philosophy: he wanted to show himself to be a great prince and the sheer volume of his possessions was a factor in this display. He came to own no fewer than sixty-three houses.

Among this great tally of houses, Greenwich, where Henry VIII was born in 1491, occupied a special place. It meant pleasure. His architectural contribution to the palace built by his father consisted of kennels, stables, tennis courts, a cockpit, a tiltyard with distinctive towers for storming in mock combats, and armour workshops – as well, it must be said, as the rebuilding of the chapel. Always impatient, he insisted on these works being rushed up with all speed. When a banqueting house was built in 1527, the workmen laboured throughout the night, working by the light of candles.

One of the attractions of Greenwich was its relative accessibility, thanks to its position on the river. Henry travelled there by barge, and his gaily caparisoned oarsmen must have made a fine sight, as they took the King down the river. Shortly after the divorce from Catherine of Aragon, Anne Boleyn was escorted from Greenwich to the Tower, four miles away, by a flotilla of barges of the Crafts of London, 'deckyd', as Archbishop Cranmer wrote in a letter, 'after the most gorgiouse and sumptuous maner'. The journey was accompanied by the blaring of trumpets and other instruments, 'as combly donne as neuer was lyke in any tyme nyghe to our rememberaunce'. Guns fired a salute for the length of the way. It was by river, too, that most of the building materials arrived. The weather could be an impediment: in February 1517 the Venetian ambassador was prevented from going to Greenwich because the river had frozen. In 1536 the King and Queen Jane were forced to ride from London to Greenwich for the same reason.

In moving between his large number of residences, Henry VIII was following the practice of all English monarchs since William the Conqueror. He would descend upon his farther-flung properties, as well as the houses of his courtiers, during the summer, as part of a progress around his realm to show himself to his people. In the winter, the court shifted in a random pattern between the different houses around London, of which Greenwich was one. There were various reasons for this, one being to thoroughly clean those that had recently been vacated. The winter movements followed a previously prepared timetable known as the 'giest'. This could be interrupted by the great dread that the King had of plague. The court would decamp as soon as an outbreak occurred in the vicinity of where they were staying, or alter course if any case had been found near their intended destination.

Part of the principle of magnificence was that the pleasures enjoyed by Henry VIII at Greenwich and elsewhere should generally be taken in public. Jousting, maying, dancing, feasting, hunting – these activities, which Henry certainly loved, often had a ceremonial importance that went hand in hand with the personal enjoyment they afforded. Those that did not were invested with an elaborate symbolism, sometimes gratuitous, sometimes overworked, but radiating the values with which Henry wanted his name to be associated. They focused on chivalry. The age of knight errantry, if it ever existed, was at, or beyond, its last gasp. Warfare was becoming an increasingly indiscrimate activity as a result of gunpowder. The last battle in which knights had ridden to the field in full armour had been Flodden in 1513. But it was the golden age of chivalry that provided the visual language for the pageantry of his court.

On May Day in 1515 Queen Catherine led a cavalcade of nobles, ambassadors and ladies, all richly dressed, out of Greenwich to meet the King and a hundred noblemen in a wood, probably on

Shooters Hill. There were twenty-five damsels to accompany the Queen, all riding white ponies. The King and his party wore green and carried bows, as though they were foresters or possibly Robin Hood. This scene was watched by an enormous crowd, said to have numbered twenty-five thousand people. Folk must have thought it was worth travelling some distance to watch the pageant. On another occasion, the populace made such a press that they were able to tear the costly robes and golden embellishments off the courtiers' backs, even stripping the King 'into his hosen and doublet'; the guard came quickly to prevent further loss of apparel. Part of chivalry was courtly love which dignified the King's infidelities. Duke Humphrey's Tower, now repaired and named Mireflore, was convenient for amorous purposes.

A Tudor palace was essentially a theatre. When the King and his court were not there to people the rooms, they would have been empty and almost bare of decoration. The King's rich furniture, gaily coloured tapestries and other signs of opulence preceded him from house to house. There is a similarly theatrical quality about many of the events and practices which happened there. Even the washing of the King's hands before eating, with water brought by noblemen of high degree, was a matter of ritual and display. Many of the entertainments were carefully planned and staged. They made a tremendous impression, at a time when reports of such happenings were sent around Europe by letter. One series of reports has survived in the archives of Venice, thanks to the assiduous correspondence of successive Venetian ambassadors and secretaries. They offer the best description of Tudor Greenwich that can be found.

Naturally the Venetian reports concentrate on great occasions of state, such as the betrothal in 1514 of Henry VIII's sister Mary, then a radiant girl of sixteen, to Louis XII of France, age sixty-two, represented for the occasion by the Duke of Longueville. The ceremony took place in a chamber on the first floor, hung with cloth of gold that was embroidered with the royal arms. The betrothal of the future Queen Mary, Henry's three-year-old daughter, to the Dauphin of France in 1518 was even more sumptuous. Cardinal Wolsey placed a ring set with a large diamond on her finger, and the Lord Admiral of France passed it over the second joint. The little girl is supposed to have lisped: 'Are you the Dauphin of France? If you are, I wish to kiss you.' Two days later a joust was held, followed by a grand supper. The Venetian ambassador noted the precise number of gold vessels: thirty-two vases, the smallest being a foot high, and four drinking glasses that were two foot high.

Even these celebrations were outdone when the Emperor Charles V came to Greenwich in 1522. The palace was crammed with people, but there was still not enough room. Some of the Emperor's retinue had to be billeted on townspeople. It suggests the scale of Greenwich at this time that there were twenty-seven dwellings of sufficient amenity to accommodate them. The Vicarage took four guests, 'The Syne of the Greyhound' (presumably an inn) put up ten. Several houses had been built alongside the palace, by courtiers wanting something more by way of privacy than palace lodgings could offer.

Given the theatrical temper of the court, it is not surprising that Henry should have delighted in stage productions, such as pageants and the new Italian fashion of masques. When these took place, tiers of benches would be lined up either side of a hall; in front of each bench was a bar of wood that spectators could lean on as they watched the performance. These productions would involve courtiers, the gentlemen being masked. At the end of the dance with which they would finish, the men would take off their masks to reveal that – to everyone's incomplete astonishment – one of them had been the King. On one occasion the floor on which this took place is described as having been laid with cloth embroidered with gold lilies. 'Some of the damsels are so beautiful as to be supposed goddesses rather than human beings,' wrote Gasparo Spinelli, the Venetian secretary in London.

Henry VIII 'had great physical powers' when he came to the throne and loved to exercise them. His favourite sport as a young man was jousting, or tilting, which combined drama and adrenalin in equal measure. Two knights on heavy horses, their gay caparisons flying, thundered towards each other in full armour, each with the object of breaking the other knight's lance. It was thrilling – and dangerous – for the competitors, colourful for the spectators, the whole thing wrapped up in the chivalric values by which Henry VIII was so entranced. Sometimes Henry would joust every day. Tilting could only take place at the palaces which had the necessary tiltyard and stabling, so the King gave them preference in the early years of his reign. Later, when a lance had splintered inside his helmet and a heavy fall had left him concussed, he became more enamoured of tennis, which could also be played at smaller, relatively more private houses. But for tilting, Greenwich was supreme. Before Henry's time, the structures provided for tournaments – principally a grandstand for the royal party – were all temporary affairs, run up for the occasion. At Greenwich, Henry built a permanent tiltyard, overlooked by a viewing gallery and two tall towers of brick, seen rising high above the other palace buildings in early representations. It dates from 1514; there was also to be a tiltyard at Hampton Court, based on the one at Greenwich, but it took so long to finish that it was never used in his lifetime.

Armour was a necessity for jousting, and it was at Greenwich, in the 1510s, that Henry built workshops to make it. He took a close interest in the design. In 1524 he ordered, according to Hall, 'a newe harnesse made of his owne devyse and fashion, suche as no armorer before that tyme had seen'. It was while Henry was trying this armour in a joust against his brother-in-law, the Duke of Suffolk, that the lance splintered inside Henry's helmet – an accident that could have cost him his sight or even killed him. Initially the metalworkers who made Henry VIII's armours came from Milan, but they did not stay long, their place being taken by Germans. As deftly jointed as a lobster's tail, their armours, hammered out on anvils known as the Great and Little Bear, were diapered and damascened with decorative flourishes, and sometimes inlaid with gold. For all that, they never reached the extremes of fantasy and elaboration seen in some continental work: relatively speaking these were sober suits.

When Henry VIII was twenty-one, and had just been enjoying a period of 'Solemptne Justes' at Greenwich, he ordered all his ships

Left **Seating plan for the banquet at Greenwich on 7 July 1517.** *Right* **Score card for the tournament of May 1516. Blows to the head, to the upper body and broken lances are recorded, as well as the number of courses run.**

and galleys to be prepared, with all their rigging and ordnance. The soldiers who were to man them were mustered on Blackheath, and their captains appointed. This preceded a review of the fleet – the first on record – which took place at Portsmouth. Unfortunately, the Battle of Brest Haven soon followed in 1512, during which the chief ship of the English, *The Regent*, was burnt.

This concentrated Henry's mind on England's vulnerability by sea, her lack of great ships and of any but one or two ships which were permanently equipped for war. To remedy this, he established the dockyard at Deptford, adjacent to Greenwich, in 1513, and the one at Woolwich, a few miles to the east, shortly afterwards. At this period, dockyards were *ad hoc* establishments – little more than a collection of storehouses. It was therefore an innovation when John Hopton, comptroller of ships, made a pond in a meadow next to the storehouse at Deptford, constructing a dock big enough to take the ships *Great Galley, Mary Rose, Great Bark, Less Bark* and *Peter Pomegranate*. By the end of the reign Deptford had become the most important of Henry's dockyards. The dockyard at Woolwich grew up around the construction of the mighty ship which Henry commissioned after the loss of *The Regent*, the *Henri Grace de Dieu*, or *Great Harry*.

The brilliance of Henry VIII's Greenwich is caught in a verse by the antiquarian Leland, originally written in Latin:

Lo, with what lustre shines this wished for place!
Which, star-like, might the heavenly mansions grace.
What painted roofs! What windows charm the eye!
What turrets, rivals of the starry sky!
What constant springs! What verdant meads besides,
Where Flora's self in majesty resides,
And beauteous all around her does dispense,

With bounteous hand, her flow'ry influence.
Happy the man whose lucky wit could frame,
To suit this place, so elegant a name,
Expressing all its beauties in the same.

Colour, fantasy, sparkling glass and flowers – the charm reaches down to us even now, centuries after the last vestige of the buildings has disappeared.

However, the crisis of the royal divorce from Catherine of Aragon and the subsequent rupture with the Church of Rome cast their shadow over Greenwich. The glow faded from the previously rosy reports of the Venetian ambassador. With the instalment of Anne Boleyn he was moved to speak in such 'lewd fashion' of the King and his Council that he had to be recalled, making Venice without an ambassador in England for over fifty years. Before that happened, the Venetians had described what must have been a hair-raising sermon preached before the King on Easter Day 1532 by the Observant friar William Peto. Peto 'gravely reproved such as repudiate their wives, declaring that by no means can they be saved; and, although appearing to speak generally, he threatened the island with excommunication, saying that the ruin of kingdoms always proceeds from the evils of flatterers'. Henry VIII seems not to have missed the point: he rose and stalked out.

Earlier in his reign, Henry VIII had gone out of his way to praise the friars for 'their strict adherence to poverty, their sincerity, charity and devotion'. It was in their church that his marriage to Catherine of Aragon had been celebrated. She remained devoted to them, often worshipping in the friary church, sometimes at night. She appointed one of the friars to be her confessor and expressed a wish to be buried in the friary. After her departure, the existence of these poor and godly monks, just the other side of the palace wall, must have seemed a living reproof to the luxury and goings-on of the court. Worse for Henry, they were not to be silenced. And when Henry's representatives arrived to take an oath from the friars, acknowledging the King to be supreme head of the Church, every one of them refused. They were arrested or dispersed. Of those that were arrested about thirty died, some of starvation. One, after torture, was strangled with the cord of his habit.

In the second half of his reign, Henry VIII was less drawn to Greenwich. Following the ruin of Cardinal Wolsey in 1529, Henry VIII had the novelty of Hampton Court to enjoy; and given his restless nature and delight in architectural effects, this new palace, barely finished, must have seemed preferable to the one built by his father, with its uncomfortable memories and recalcitrant friars.

But Greenwich retained the love of Henry VIII's children. His son, the boy king Edward VI, enjoyed himself there, according to entries that he made in his diary in 1551 when he was fourteen: 'March 31. A chaleng made by me that I, with 16 of my chaumbre, shuld runne at base, shote, and rune at ring, with any 17 of my servauntes, gentlemen in the court.' Running at ring was an exercise performed on horses, one of many which encouraged the important accomplishment, both for wartime and everyday, of riding well. Two high posts were erected, with a small ring dangling from a crossbeam at the end of a string. Contestants had to impale the ring on the end of their lance.

Two years later Greenwich was also the scene of Edward's pathetic death. It happened not in Placentia but in the mansion of Old Court, immediately to the east of Greenwich, which the Lord Protector, the newly created Duke of Northumberland, had got out of the King. Northumberland had the consumptive boy moved from Placentia into his own house, when doctors diagnosed that he had only three days to live. Edward VI's last days were spun out by means of arsenic, which temporarily stopped the haemorrhages. It must have caused the dying King terrible pain. His hair fell out and his extremities turned gangrenous. By the time he was actually dead, the body was in such a horrifying state that it could not be shown immediately. There was a rumour that the corpse subsequently produced and buried in Westminster Abbey was not that of the King at all, but a similar-looking youth who had been murdered in his place. The distorted remains of the King, according to this version, were disposed of somewhere in Greenwich.

The whole escapade seems as improbable and grotesque as a revenge tragedy by an Elizabethan dramatist. It ended in the predictable disaster: Lady Jane Grey was Queen for ten days, imprisoned, then – following an uprising during which Sir Thomas Wyatt camped his band of rebels on Blackheath – she, her husband and members of their family were executed. Northumberland had already been beheaded on the accession of Mary Tudor.

As a Roman Catholic, Mary reinstated the friars at Greenwich, her mother's champions Peto and Elston among them. But the times had changed, and townspeople pelted them with stones. It is from Mary's reign that we are allowed our first glimpse of the royal palace of Greenwich, through two tinted drawings made by the Flemish artist Anthony Wyngaerde, who was in the employment of Philip of Spain. These are the first detailed depictions of the place, and show the great rambling length of its river frontage.

Unlike her father, Queen Elizabeth, despite her long reign, built virtually nothing. The Office of Works, responsible for royal building operations, became little more than a palace maintenance department. Still, it is a sign of her regard for Greenwich that Queen Elizabeth, so careful with her finances, spent more on it annually than on any other palace except Whitehall. It became her principal summer residence 'for the delightfulness of its situation', according to the German visitor Paul Hentzner, who travelled through England when Elizabeth was an old woman, in 1598.

There are occasional accounts of ceremonies and entertainments which took place at Greenwich during Elizabeth's reign: a muster by men-at-arms from the City of London in 1559; a water pageant, in which a mock castle was attacked by pinnaces, on Midsummer's Day 1561; the distribution of Maunday gifts, with the Queen washing the feet (previously prepared by the yeoman of the laundry and the sub-almoner with copious supplies of flower-water) of thirty-nine paupers in 1572. Generally, the pace of revelry had slowed since her father's time. But Greenwich was acquiring a new significance through its association with the great maritime adventures of the age, including the defeat of the Armada. Many names from that greatest of seafaring counties, Devon, recur in Greenwich. It is easy to see why: when Devon sailors were not fighting the Spanish, they were engaged in trade. This would have taken them to the wharves downstream of London, and some of them stayed. Sir Francis Drake's early years were spent plying along the coast in a small trading boat, sometimes crossing over to Zeeland and France, but probably more often sailing up the Thames estuary towards London. Later he joined his relation Sir John Hawkins at Deptford, and eventually it was from here that he left to circumnavigate the globe in the *Pelican*, later renamed the *Golden Hind*. After a banquet at Deptford served on board the *Golden Hind*, the Queen knighted Drake with a gilded sword. Some of the attraction of Greenwich to Queen Elizabeth must have been its proximity to Deptford, only a mile or two away. There would always have been something of interest for her to see in Deptford. It was while she was being rowed between Greenwich and Deptford that a bystander accidentally let off an arquebus, which put a bullet through both the arms of one of her oarsmen. The offender was strung up at the gallows, only to be reprieved when the noose was in place. The London merchant Henry Machyn records a mock naval battle put on for the Queen's entertainment at Deptford in 1560. Four pinnaces attacked a brigantine, with men hurled into the water, pikes and stones being thrown and 'as grett shutyng as cold be'. There were more than four thousand people present, though how many were combatants is not clear.

If the episode of Sir Walter Raleigh and his cloak, thrown down to allow Elizabeth to cross a 'plashy place' without muddying the royal shoes, took place at all, it took place at Greenwich. That at least is where Sir Walter Scott set it in his novel *Kenilworth*.

We can picture Queen Elizabeth at Greenwich, at the end of her reign, through Hentzner's detailed description of his visit. The Queen was then sixty-five, 'very majestic' as Hentzner writes: indeed the living icon that is familiar from the portraits of her. An oblong face, fair but wrinkled; small black eyes; rather a hooked nose; thin lips; and (not evident in the paintings) 'her teeth black (a defect the English seem subject to, from their too great use of sugar)' – those were her features. She was dripping with jewels, with heavy earrings, a long necklace, a small crown on top of her red wig, a collar of gold and jewels about her neck and pearls 'the size of beans' sewn onto her white silk dress. It is hardly surprising that 'her air was stately', given the weight of this garniture; for all the blaze of possessions her manner of speaking remained 'mild and obliging'.

It was a Sunday, and she was on her way to the chapel rebuilt by Henry VIII. To get there she had to pass through a throng of people. Her guard of Gentlemen Pensioners alone numbered fifty. The Presence Chamber swarmed with courtiers, including the Archbishop of Canterbury, the Bishop of London and various members of the Council. As she went along, the Queen bestowed a few words, switching easily between English, French and Italian, to the different people who had come to address her. They did so on bended knee; in fact it was etiquette for all to kneel when she turned her face towards them. The Queen was followed by some ladies, 'very handsome and well-shaped'. In the ante chapel the cry went up 'Long live Queen Elizabeth!' To which she answered: 'I thank you, my good people.'

After chapel, dinner. Not being of the inner circle, Hentzner did not see the Queen eat; even so he could witness the extraordinary ritual with which her food was prepared. It reads rather as though it were a dumb show put on for the benefit of the many visitors. It certainly impressed Hentzner, who describes it minutely:

> ... a Gentleman entered the room bearing a rod, and
> along with him another who had a table-cloth, which,
> after they had both kneeled three times with the utmost
> veneration, he spread upon the table, and, after
> kneeling again, they both retired. Then came two
> others, one with the rod again, the other with a salt-
> cellar, a plate, and bread; when they had kneeled, as the
> others had done, and placed what was brought upon
> the table, they too retired with the same ceremonies
> performed by the first.
>
> At last, came an unmarried Lady (we were told she
> was a Countess), and along with her a married one,
> bearing a tasting knife; the former was dressed in white
> silk, who, when she had prostrated herself three times
> in the most graceful manner, approached the table, and
> rubbed the plates with bread and salt, with as much awe
> as if the Queen had been present: when they had waited
> there a little while, the Yeomen of the Guard entered,

bare-headed, clothed in scarlet, with a gold rose upon their backs, bringing in at each turn a course of twenty-four dishes, served in plate, most of it gilt; these dishes were received by a gentleman in the same order they were brought, and placed upon the table, while the lady-taster gave to each of the guards a mouthful to eat, of the particular dish he had brought, for fear of any poison. During the time that this guard, which consists of the tallest and stoutest men that can be found in all England, being carefully selected for this service, were bringing dinner, twelve trumpets and two kettle-drums made the hall ring for half an hour together.

The Queen ate in a private chamber, with just a few attendants. Only after she had taken what she wanted were the dishes provided to the ladies of the court.

All those trumpets and kettle-drums indicate the importance that music had for the Elizabethan court. There was a great call for musicians, who performed for dancing, pageants and plays as well as the religious services. Among the Gentlemen of the Chapel, as the musicians attached to the Chapel Royal were known, was the composer Thomas Tallis. Like many of the musicians, he chose Greenwich as his home and in 1585 was buried in the parish church.

The musicians were not tied to Greenwich but many of them made their home there. Several generations of Laniers, Ferraboscos, Mells and Comeys – all families of musicians – appear in the parish register. There was also a boys' choir attached to the court, and these Children of the Chapel had their home at Greenwich. We can imagine them, perhaps, singing in Shakespeare's production of his own *Midsummer-Night's Dream*, given there in 1594.

Clearly the royal presence at Placentia helped stimulate development of the town, as well as lending an air of fashion to the neighbourhood. The area continued to attract city merchants, such as the linen draper John Lambarde who bought the manor of Westcombe, just east of Placentia. His son William, who was a lawyer, wrote the first history of Kent. It was a long time after his father's death in 1554 before William Lambarde could fully enter into his inheritance at Westcombe, because of a dispute with his younger brother. William also founded the almshouses called Queen Elizabeth's College in 1575. It was the first public charity to have been established since the Reformation, as well as the first of a series of charities to be bestowed upon Greenwich. The original almshouses were rebuilt in the Elizabethan manner in 1819, and are the first sight of Greenwich for visitors arriving by train, as they stand opposite the station.

William Lambarde's antiquarian bent was recognised by Queen Elizabeth, who made him Master of the Rolls (the Rolls Chapel being the forerunner of the present Public Record Office) and Keeper of the Records in the Tower of London. One morning in 1601 he visited her at Placentia, to present a copy of his *Account of the Records of the Tower*. It is intriguing to imagine this meeting between two old people, one of them preoccupied by history as represented in old documents, the other a figure of history in her own right. They discussed a picture of Richard II which Baron Lumley (himself an obsessive antiquarian where his own pedigree was concerned) had found nailed to a basement wall in his house and then given to the Queen.

It was not long before both the antiquarian and the old Queen were dead; and with the departure of the stilted figures of the Elizabethan court Greenwich entered another era, projecting it into the vanguard of architectural taste.

LOVE AND KINDNESS INCREASE DAILY BETWEEN THEM

I N APRIL 1603, King James VI of Scotland, soon to be crowned also James I of England, began his journey from Edinburgh to his new capital of London. He had travelled to Denmark before, in a rather rash undertaking to bring back his bride, Anne, the Danish King's fifteen-year-old daughter, in person (there had been such stormy seas that the superstitious James thought that witches had been working spells on him). But he had never so much as set foot in the country over which he would reign. So he was as curious to see England, as he journeyed south, as his new subjects were to see him. First he entered Berwick, where 'he was receved with great ioy as kinge', according to Sir Roger Wilbraham, who had served Elizabeth I in various official positions and would receive preferment under James. All his way he was met 'with great solemnity and state', everywhere being greeted by large troops of horsemen, waited on by sheriffs and gentlemen, presented with orations and gifts, and generally entertained with as much show as the neighbourhood could muster.

People streamed from London to see their new King arrive at Robert Cecil's house Theobalds in Hertfordshire, so many that a private road had to be quickly made to let him through. Even larger crowds assembled along the remainder of the route. About four miles from London James was welcomed by the Lord Mayor and 'such unspeakable nomber of citizens, as the like nomber was never seene to issue out upon any cause before'. Finally he reached the Charterhouse in the City of London, where he stayed for four nights, before decamping to the Tower to escape the ever-present throng, going out secretly by coach or barge to view London, the Palace of Whitehall and the jewels there. But his incognito did not do him much good; he found himself besieged by a multitude of hopefuls who thought that their best chance of receiving a royal favour was to strike while the iron was hot, endlessly swarming 'about his maiestie at every back gate & privie dore to his great offence'. So after four days at the Tower he announced that anyone who hoped for a knighthood would have to wait until the coronation, and removed to Greenwich.

Greenwich came to assume an important place in James's affections even though it did not possess quite the associations for him that it had for his predecessor. James enjoyed nothing so much as the country life. He spoke of London as 'that filthie toune'. Hunting was his greatest diversion: a poor physical specimen who could not walk very well, he became a different man on a horse, and spent so many hours in the saddle that little else could get done. There were complaints that he neglected official business, but James did not care. He argued that it was good for his constitution, and it was essential to the well-being of the nation that it had a healthy king. Greenwich was the nearest place to London where he could hunt. It was not the best place: that was to be found on the borders of Cambridge and Hertfordshire, around Theobalds and Royston. He also had a preference for Newmarket where he established one of many racecourses. Still, sport at Greenwich was not to be overlooked. It came into its own, however, in the spring, when the hunting had finished, and the Hertfordshire and Cambridgeshire houses were shut up. Then James established a 'standing' or semi-permanent court at Greenwich, whose country airs he much preferred to Whitehall.

In that first year of his reign, this pattern of occupation lay in the future. James was content, to begin with, just to survey his new possessions. On 22 May, Giovanni Carlo Scaramelli, the Venetian Secretary in England, reported that the six men-of-war and two armed pinnaces which Elizabeth had commissioned before her death were being sailed down to Greenwich for James to inspect.

Altogether, in the English context, James was an oddity who could hardly have seemed more different from Elizabeth I. Contemporaries knew the Queen as being a 'comely' woman, with a strong constitution, who was 'solemn and ceremonious', rigid in her ideas about the hierarchy that constituted social order, parsimonious, utterly majestic in her bearing but prepared to speak to strangers and 'her people' when they came her way. James, by contrast, was not well made: his legs had been bent through rickets, so he liked to lean on the shoulder of one of his courtiers when he walked. His tongue, we are told in a spiteful account, was too big for his mouth, which made him apt to spill his drink and food as he ate. In contrast to the ossified stiffness that had turned his predecessor into a living icon, James had no regard for convention, and his offhand manner and sometimes curious choice of clothes were apt to make him appear slightly ludicrous. Both Queen Elizabeth and King James had their favourites, but the word took on a different connotation at the Jacobean court: James, this funny-looking man, brought up in a world of extreme violence, often in danger of his life, educated under the aegis of the dour Scottish Calvinist George Buchanan, felt an emotional pull towards the sort of dashing young men whose passage through life seemed so much easier than his own.

He became besotted with one after another of them. He behaved in a physically affectionate manner towards them in public; no one knows what happened in private but it is assumed that the intimacies were taken further. He heaped them with favours: it reflected a nature that was naturally generous. Whereas Elizabeth had been 'strict in her giving, which age and her sex inclined her unto', James disregarded the precarious state of the royal finances and gave with both hands. He indulged others, and he indulged himself. Corruption was second nature to the sycophants who surrounded the King. Everything was for sale, including peerages and the specially created title of baronet. The court became a byword for licentiousness, duplicity, greed, reckless extravagance, triviality and self-interest. 'Here I am tied about my own business,' wrote Sir Henry Wootton from Greenwich Palace to a friend in 1611, 'which I have told you like a true courtier; for right courtiers indeed have no other business but themselves.'

It is worth dwelling on the tone of the Jacobean court, set by the King himself; for out of it emerged the first of the Greenwich masterpieces that we can see and visit for ourselves – the Queen's House. Nothing, apparently, could form a greater contrast with the debauchery, ostentation and venality that typified the court; but then James himself was something more, too. For a monarch he was formidably learned, a King who loved bookish conversation, was an authority on witchcraft (it was probably to flatter him that Shakespeare included witches in his patently James-pleasing *Macbeth*), instigated the Authorised Version of the Bible and himself wrote tracts such as the presciently anti-smoking pamphlet *Counterblaste to Tobacco*. Furthermore, Greenwich came to be associated more and more with his Queen, Anne of Denmark; eventually he gave it to her, though he continued to use it as well; and it is her personality which finally pervaded it.

The martyrdom of St Alfege, twelfth-century window from Canterbury Cathedral.
Alfege, Archbishop of Canterbury, was killed by Danish invaders at Greenwich.

The Peasants' Revolt, 1381.
Blackheath provided a convenient
open space for the rabble led by Wat
Tyler and Jack Straw to assemble,
before descending on London.

Above Queen Elizabeth dancing La Volta with the Earl of Leicester. The musicians are probably Alfonso Ferrabosco, Caesar Galliardello and Richard Farrant and John Lanier, all of whom lived at Greenwich.

Left Henry VIII on board the *Henri Grace de Dieu*, or *Great Harry*. It was built at the dockyard which the King established at Woolwich, near Greenwich.

Following pages Detail from *A View of Greenwich Park*, by Adriaen Van Stalbemt and Jan Van Belcamp, 1632. Charles I and Henrietta Maria appear in the foreground with their family and courtiers.

Inigo Jones, painted by William Hogarth after Van Dyke. Painter, masque designer, antiquarian, connoisseur and architect, Jones blazed a meteoric path through the courts of James I and Charles I.

Anne was an easygoing woman, certainly not erudite like her husband, but (according to some sources) intelligent, wise enough to stay out of the mess that was James's government, without being unaware of it. Above all she was what would now be called a party animal. 'She likes enjoyment and is very fond of dancing and of fetes,' reported Nicolo Molin, the Venetian ambassador, in 1607, when she was twenty-three. England was said to have a hunting King and a dancing Queen. She had been pretty as a girl; interminable pregnancies and miscarriages, as well as the disappointments of her marriage, took their toll, and by the time she came to Greenwich she had lost her looks. Her ladies knew her, rather engagingly, as Rina, a contraction of Regina. She seems to have had a kind nature. Not surprisingly, given the King's preoccupation with hunting as well as his weakness for male favourites, the King and Queen were not always in each other's company. Nevertheless, as their last child, Sophia, was born in 1607, they evidently continued to have sexual relations beyond what might be considered the call of duty (they had already secured the succession by producing three boys).

In all respects, the Jacobean history of Greenwich reflects the feelings of affection that seemed to exist within this baffling royal marriage. There had been a curious incident at Theobalds in July 1613, when the court had been hunting. The Queen took aim at a deer, but instead shot Jewel, the King's favourite hound. There could hardly have been a worse offence in James's canon of values than so unfortunate an interference with his hunting (he was implacable in his severity against poachers). No one can have been very surprised that, as Master John Chamberlain wrote to his friend Sir Dudley Carleton, 'he stormed exceedingly awhile'. But the anger abated, and he assured her not to be upset by it, 'for he should love her never the worse'. The next day he sent her a diamond of immense worth (£2,000) as a legacy from the deceased Jewel. 'Love and kindness increase daily between them,' continued Chamberlain; 'and it is thought they never were on better terms.' James was someone who did not wish unduly to distress those close to him, so long as he could do what he wanted. So he responded generously to what seems to have been a more emollient attitude towards his favourites on Anne's part. On 25 November 1613, Chamberlain could report: 'the Queen by her late pacification hath gained Greenwich into jointure.' In other words the King gave Anne the palace to which she had become particularly attached. His generosity was all the more remarkable in view of the possessions that she had already received at the time of his entry into Britain: Denmark House (later Somerset House) in London and Oatlands in Surrey.

The King was not the sole provider of the Queen's lavish gift. Henry Howard, Earl of Northampton and founder of Trinity Hospital, had built one of the great courtier houses near Placentia. Brought up at Greenwich, Northampton became Keeper of the Game in Greenwich Park and amassed enormous possessions at Greenwich, some of which he was forced to surrender to the Queen. Unlike most noblemen of his age, Northampton was a formidable scholar, fluent in many languages and deeply learned in history, theology and philosophy. Such talents found expression in his splendid new house – 'my mistress,' as he tenderly referred to it – which his great-nephew, Thomas Howard, Earl of Arundel inherited upon his death in 1614.

Arundel maintained and expanded Northampton's lavish attention to the 'mistress'. It seems that he started collecting art soon after inheriting the Greenwich house, going on to become one of the greatest collectors and patrons in English history. It was in this Greenwich house that his vast art collection was housed. In 1617 disaster struck. George, Lord Carew, wrote: 'The Erle of Northampton's new-built house at Greenwich (by the negligence of servants) is burnt all but the gallerye to the ground, wherein the Erle of Arundell, whose house it was, lost a great part of his householde stuffe, which was of great value.'

Northampton's lasting memorial in Greenwich was Trinity Hospital, otherwise Norfolk College, founded in 1613. With an income of £600 a year, it provided relief and maintenance for twelve poor men of the parish of East Greenwich, as well as eight poor men from Norfolk, where the founder was born. The building stands beside the river, east of the Seamen's Hospital. Originally the building comprised a chapel, a council room, four rooms for the use of the warden, a room each for the poor men, a common hall, kitchen, wash-house, brewhouse, and two rooms each for the butler, cook and female assistant.

Greenwich had acquired something of a reputation for healthiness. It had been one of the places to which Henry VIII had repaired to escape the plague, and so it remained for the new dynasty. But it also seems generally to have been associated with the benefits of a change of air. Certainly this would seem to have been the opinion of Robert Burton, author of *The Anatomy of Melancholy*, who regarded 'variety of actions, objects, air' and 'places' as being 'excellent good' in treating melancholy. He quotes Barclay the Scot's commendation of 'Greenwich tower for one of the best prospects in Europe, to see London on the one side, the Thames, ships and pleasant meadows on the other'.

Admittedly, in early December 1610 the Queen found she did not like the air at Greenwich that winter, and with some reason: a week later her friend Lady Drummond had died, it was feared of plague, and a few days later one of her companions was also taken off. Plague, however, could strike anywhere. Five years later, when the Queen was ill, her doctors and the King urged her to take the baths at Greenwich, where she accordingly went. She seems never

This 1796 engraving of Trinity Hospital shows the original elegant setting; it is now overshadowed by the Greenwich Power Station.

actually to have entered the baths, because, as the Venetian ambassador reported, 'some of the physicians thought that she ought to be half covered, while the others said it should be up to her neck, so that in consequence of this difference in opinion she had abstained'. It was to Greenwich that she went to have those of her children that were born in England.

On at least a couple of St George's Days, James held the Garter ceremonies at Greenwich, with all the knights assembling, as now happens each year at Windsor. He enjoyed the pleasures of cockfighting, bull-baiting and bear-baiting, to which the Queen was equally attached. Gambling was also part of the appeal of these blood sports. Among the salaries disbursed at Greenwich, according to a 'true collection of the fees and offices of his Majesty' drawn up in 1618, were those to the Keeper of the Park, the Keeper of the Wardrobe and the Keeper of the Lodge, Meadow and Garden. The Keeper of the Wardrobe had a particular importance, given James's excessive vanity for clothes. Perhaps it was for this reason that he set up a silk factory near Greenwich at Lewisham.

A detail of the garden at Greenwich emerges from an account of a contretemps between the future Charles I, aged sixteen, and the King's favourite George Villiers, who would become Duke of Buckingham. He would become Charles's favourite too, but as a boy Charles had hated him. Charles, Villiers and James I were standing together by a statue of Bacchus at Greenwich; it happened to be one of those novelty fountains which the overdressed aristocrats of seventeenth-century Europe found hilarious. By surreptitiously turning a pin, water could be made to spurt out suddenly and soak unsuspecting bystanders. Villiers was standing in just the right place, and the temptation for the royal youngster proved too much: 'the water spouted in Sir George Villiers his face, whereat he was very much offended,' wrote Sir Edward Sherburn to Sir Dudley

Carleton: 'the king observing his discontentment was so exceedingly moved against the Prince for doing it, as besides the hard words he gaue him, which was that he had a malicious and dogged disposicion, gaue his Highnes 2 boxes in the eare.'

On 21 June 1617, John Chamberlain wrote to Sir Dudley Carleton: 'The Queen is building somewhat at Greenwich wch must be finished this sommer, yt is saide to be some curious devise of Inigo Jones, and will cost above 4000li.' The painter, masque designer, antiquarian, connoisseur and now architect and Surveyor of the King's Works Inigo Jones had been blazing his meteoric way through the half-light of the Jacobean court for a dozen or so years. He must have dazzled and astounded contemporaries; as one might expect, this did not always make them love him, and the accounts that have come down of him – notably the lampoons made by Ben Jonson after the pair had fallen out – suggest that he was mightily full of himself. 'Huomo vanissimo e molto vantatore,' concluded an Italian, having watched him pronounce on some of Charles I's newly arrived Italian paintings. An impression of vanity is not entirely excluded from Van Dyck's memorable portrait drawing of him, though this suggests many other qualities too, such as intelligence, refinement and spirit. He is shown with his eyes straining to discern some distant vision. Contemporaries seem to have thought of him as arrogant, and it would hardly be surprising if he was: to achieve anything new in architecture requires self-confidence. A double dose must have been needed given the chaotic finances of the Stuart court. Perhaps the most surprising thing is that so little was written about Jones. He was prominent at the highest levels of the court, friendly with kings and queens. Van Dyck's record is enough to show that he must, in all senses, have cut a striking figure. His name alone – Inigo is very unusual – might have made him stand out. Yet he was invisible to the diarists and letter-writers on whom historians depend for court gossip. Maybe he adapted himself so well to his environment that they did not notice him.

Jones was the son of a London clothworker. How it was that he transcended his modest background to become such a figure of taste is a mystery. In his twenties he travelled in Italy for several years. He was not rich and we do not know how he supported himself. Perhaps he hitched himself to the train of a nobleman. By some means he entered the service of King Christian IV of Denmark, not yet twenty and brother of the English Queen. It was an unlikely milieu for this man of refinement to be happy in: the booziness of Christian IV's entourage scandalised English observers when he visited London in 1606 – though it has to be said, on that occasion, that Danish misbehaviour was equalled by James I and his court. Before long Jones was back in his native land, having transferred from the service of the brother to that of the sister. His first work for Anne of Denmark was to stage a court masque.

The masque was not an entirely new phenomenon: we have seen that Henry VIII acted in masques at Greenwich. But in the Jacobean and Caroline courts it reached a zenith of sophistication, technical complexity and symbolic meaning. It was a form of entertainment that particularly delighted the Queen. There was something of the pantomime about it, with an emphasis on outlandish costumes and seemingly magical transformations of scene. The best masques, though, must also have been very beautiful. Certainly they were lavishly expensive: for the price of some productions it would have been possible to build a country house. And they could be erudite too. A number were written by Ben Jonson, in classicising vein. Words, however, took second place to dance. The object of the masque was to demonstrate the virtues of the monarch, in an entertainment in which the court itself participated through dancing. At one point the masquers would dance and take partners from the court, dissolving the barrier between the ideal, as represented on stage, and the real, as embodied in the audience. With its arcane symbolism, it reflects the growing insularity of the court. For these revels were mounted for the royal family's and their courtiers' own delectation, without any thought of impressing the people beyond. To take a prominent part in the staging of masques was certain to attract the attention of the King and Queen, and Jones seems to have been friendly with, in particular, Charles I. By then he was established. At the beginning of his career, masque design gave him a way of demonstrating the ideas he had developed through contact with Italy, without committing his patrons to the cost of building a palace.

Only one masque was ever presented at Greenwich during James I's reign. Called *Pan's Anniversary, or the Shepherds' Holiday*, it was performed on the occasion of James I's birthday in 1620. The pastoral theme was, perhaps, appropriate to the out-of-town setting.

The spirit of the masque penetrates the extraordinary building known, after Anne of Denmark, as the Queen's House. Today it is difficult to appreciate the impression that this little villa, with its sparse decoration and rectangular profile, must have had on contemporaries. Our eyes have become habituated to the hundreds of similar structures that came after it – generally, such was its originality, long after it. But seventeenth-century England had literally seen nothing like it. It was begun in 1616, and by then Jones had made a second trip to Italy, in the train of the young Earl of Arundel who was to become one of the greatest collectors and patrons in English history. Jones was by no means exclusively interested in architecture: a sketchbook suggests that he was perhaps more concerned to study the Italian Mannerist painters whose work he admired. Nevertheless, he bought architectural textbooks, notably the *Quattro Libri* of Palladio, and set out to visit the buildings illustrated in them; he also met Palladio's disciple Vincenzo Scamozzi. It would have been enough to turn him away from the provincial style of English architecture, with its encrustations of ornament. He did not respond to the richness of Mannerism or the baroque, the 'aboundance ... brought in by Michill Angell', preferring the severity of the ancient ruins and 'the sollid, proporsionable ... and unaffected' style of Andrea Palladio. But there is nothing even among the serene country villas of Palladio that equates to the austerity of the Queen's House. The only explanation is that it emerged from Jones's study of the theory of architecture, in the works of Leon Battista Alberti and others. Jones did not borrow a fashion from Italy, he used the principles he discovered there to invent his own. So the Queen's House is not only completely unlike anything that had previously been constructed in England, but has no real parallel anywhere else in Europe either.

From 1613 Jones had been Surveyor to the King's Works (he had previously, for two years, served as Surveyor to Henry, Prince of Wales, who died in 1612). It was a remarkable appointment since Jones had yet to prove himself as capable of constructing anything very substantial. Admittedly the post was largely a matter of administering the repair of palaces and the preparations necessary to put them in readiness for the King and Queen. But it shows the favour he had come to enjoy at court, and the confidence that was placed in him. Confidence was again needed to give Jones the commission of the Queen's House. All that he had actually built by this time was a church monument in Shropshire and some outbuildings at James's Newmarket Palace. So in every respect the Queen's House was a novelty. Clearly this was how it struck contemporaries, to judge from John Chamberlain's reference to the Queen's House as being 'some curious devise'. One feature that fully justifies this description is the plan. Built on the site of the old gatehouse mentioned in Gille

Delaporte's report to the Abbot of Ghent, more than three hundred years before, it took the form of an H, the downstrokes of which stood either side of the London to Dover road, with the crossbar forming a bridge at first-floor level. Quite why the Queen wanted the road to pass through the middle of her house is unclear. It cannot have been very convenient, particularly given the value which the royal family placed on privacy. The idea that it provided a means of passing from the palace precincts into the park beyond without the indignity of walking across the public road does not seem justification enough (they could have constructed a tunnel). There is a little, perhaps, of Raleigh's cloak about it: the building provided a permanent means of keeping the Queen's feet dry.

The reason why the Queen wanted this charming box to be built there at all is no more certain. It was at the bottom of the gardens, some way from the palace, yet seclusion could not really have been the motive, given its position relative to the road. At least some of the 'curious' quality of the house derived from its being a caprice. The whimsy would have been very much to the taste of someone as enraptured with court masques as Anne. The other architectural works at Greenwich of which we hear at this period seem to spring almost directly from the world of the masque. Duke Humphrey's Tower was yet again transformed, this time into what the Venetian ambassador Pietro Contarini called 'the fabled tower of Oriana'. Near the palace itself, deliberately within earshot, was built a new aviary, through whose tall windows, covered with copper nets, birdsong poured forth. Very much in the spirit of *Pan's Anniversary*.

One explanation might lie in the nature of some forms of hunting in the seventeenth century. Hunting could involve participants, such as James, in long, invigorating and almost addictive hours in the saddle; but there were also more formalised versions that did not entail much galloping over the countryside, at least on the part of the principal spectators, since the game – hare or deer – was coursed by dogs along a designated track, conveniently placed in full sight of a building that served as a viewing platform. It is likely that the Queen's House was intended to serve as a grandstand, both for hunting and military parades. As built, the side facing the Park has a loggia which would have done very well for this purpose. It is also possible that the Queen's House was conceived, from the start, as a place to receive important visitors whose first impression of Britain would have been Greenwich. There is more evidence from the reign of Charles I that suggests this intention.

The Queen's House has come to be regarded as the *fons et origo* of all Classical architecture in Britain. One aspect of this is the harmony of the proportions, achieved through numerical relationships. This had been a prominent element in the architectural theory of Palladio. Contemporaries were much struck by Jones's preoccupation with numbers: Ben Jonson ridiculed him for it. To anyone steeped in the culture of Renaissance Italy, it would have seemed self-evident that spaces based on pure geometry pleased the eye and engendered a feeling of equilibrium. Jones had imbibed this idea during his travels, and he applied it by designing an exactly cubic hall for the Queen's House. One wonders whether this was how all Jones's patrons saw it. Perhaps the Jacobean court, presided over by a King who was intensely superstitious, responded differently to the magic of numbers. Did they picture Inigo Jones's number theory as leading them forward, towards an age of harmony and humanism, or as harking back to the medieval world of sorcery to which some of them were still attached? Certainly the Queen's House was a wonder and a mystery – and so it remains. The mystery is due in part to Anne's death in 1619, before the house had been finished.

* * *

76

In about 1632, Adriaen Van Stalbemt and Jan Van Belcamp painted an elegant view of Greenwich. It shows a hunting scene. In the foreground, sublimely detached from the activities of the chase, Charles I, wearing a black broad-brimmed hat and with a cloak thrown over one shoulder, escorts his Queen, the dark-eyed summation of elegance Henrietta Maria, to the top of a slight rise in the Park. She holds the hand of her daughter. It is an affecting image, painted at a time when the King and Queen, after a disastrous start to their marriage, had come, quite publicly and against convention, to love each other very much. They are not alone. They are not surrounded by the great press of people who might have mobbed one of the Tudor monarchs, but a select band of courtiers. To the left of the royal group stand a couple talking pleasantly between themselves. The younger of the two, with his hand on his hip and a smile ruffling the moustaches of his pointed beard, is Endymion Porter, a gallant who was as colourful as his name, having been one of the two trusted friends to accompany Charles, then Prince of Wales, and the dazzling Marquis of Buckingham on their madcap, incognito dash to Madrid to woo (unsuccessfully) the Infanta Maria, sister to the King of Spain, in 1623; subsequently it was Porter who made the first of Charles's overtures to the painter Sir Anthony Van Dyck, which would end in the latter's residing in England. The other, more soberly if still fashionably clad, wearing a close-fitting cap, is none other than Inigo Jones. In the middle distance behind them can be seen the Queen's House, with the Park wall extending to either side of it, but complete only up to the first floor and thatched over at that level – the state in which it was left on Anne's death and for the next ten years.

Much had happened in the thirteen years since Anne of Denmark's death. The desperate state of the royal finances had been revealed by the delay that took place before the pomps of her funeral could be staged – her body lay unburied for ten weeks. Inigo Jones designed the immense catafalque, in the manner of Bramante's *Tempietto*, erected in Westminster Abbey for James's own obsequies in 1625. With his death the court sounded a different note, which resonated, as much as anywhere, at Greenwich.

The court of James I had been 'a nursery of lust and intemperance … and every greate house in the country became a sty of uncleanesse'. So wrote the Puritan critic Mrs Hutchinson. But even she had to admit that the Caroline court was a different place. 'The face of the court was much chang'd in the change of the king; for King Charles was temperate, chast and serious. … The nobility and courtiers, who did not quite abandon their debosheries, had yet that reverence to the king to retire into corners to practise them.' Who can say what corners were provided by Greenwich? What comes down to us from Charles's reign, in the completion of the Queen's House, is witness only to the culture and elegance of the court.

There is a painting in the National Maritime Museum at Greenwich which shows the palace from the north side of the river. It suggests that, in the newly elegant age, Greenwich had become a place of fashionable resort, where sophisticated couples might stroll side by side along the bank of the Thames, albeit under the gaze, in this case, of a peasant woman and her child. The foreground of the picture shows a rowing boat bearing more elegantly dressed people. Skiffs dart across the water: the activity on the river must have been constant. But the most imposing sight is that of a fine man-of-war at anchor, its St George's flag beating proudly in the breeze. The artist is unidentified, but clearly Flemish. With, apparently, one exception – the entirely unexplained inclusion of another great house on the left of the painting – the picture is topographically accurate. If it is accurate in the style of life represented, we can conclude that the charms of Greenwich had been discovered by a wider spectrum of people than just the court. On such a day as that depicted, it must have been a joy to make an outing along the river there. It was painted about 1630, just as work on the Queen's House had recommenced.

The change at court had not happened suddenly at James's death. For some years before that date the old King, tired and senile, had virtually surrendered the governance of the country to the Prince of Wales and the now Duke of Buckingham. The favourite whom Charles had once hated he now adored. And as much as the young Prince, soon to be King, loved this captivating, greedy, impossibly sumptuous man, his young bride, understandably, hated him.

Charles had married Henrietta Maria in 1624. She was no more than a girl, the youngest daughter of Henri IV of France, and came to England with a very large retinue of attendants, determined to adapt as little as possible to the ways of her new country. To begin with, married life was a disaster. But matters improved after the King, normally so courteous, felt himself to be driven beyond endurance, and expelled Henrietta Maria's compatriots. Their departure showed them for what they were, since they plundered all of their young mistress's possessions that they could lay hands on. Charles's masterfulness at last made Henrietta Maria respect him. She may have reflected that, without her own court, it was in her own interests to submit to his will, since Cardinal Richelieu had no wish to see her back in France. Then in 1628 the Duke of Buckingham was stabbed to death, just as her own father had been. Devastated by the loss, Charles turned to her. She did what she could to console him. From that moment grew the love that united them in a dangerous and finally tragic destiny. One of its first expressions seems to have been a resumption of work on the Queen's House at Greenwich. Charles gave Greenwich, so long associated with English queens, to Henrietta Maria the year after

Buckingham was murdered. That same year Henrietta Maria was at Greenwich, in preparation for the birth of her first child.

Since Queen Anne's death, Charles had been in possession of Greenwich. He used it in the summer of 1619: we know that from a surviving letter dated from Greenwich in June that year. It had been intended that the palace would have been one of the first places Henrietta Maria saw on arriving at Dover: the plan had been to travel more or less straight there, by way of Canterbury. This had not proved to be possible because of plague. Perhaps it might have made a more favourable impression on the young Queen and her entourage than the one they formed, coloured by what they regarded as the meanness of their reception (there was no money for splendid ceremonies). During the disastrous war with Spain in 1626, Charles had watched with gratification as a large and heavily laden 'berton', a type of merchantman, owned by Hamburgers trading with England's enemy, was brought up the river, following its capture by an English ship. It must have been one of the few episodes of that misconceived campaign to give him any pleasure. Charles and Henrietta Maria followed precedent by making a stay at Greenwich a regular feature of the early summer months.

It was some years into their marriage before Henrietta Maria became pregnant for the first time, and she had become anxious at the delay. When that happy state came upon her, she retired, in accordance with royal tradition, to Greenwich. Everything seemed to be well as she entered the sixth month of her pregnancy. She was walking in the Park: indeed that exercise, particularly since it was apt to be taken up-hill, was one of many causes to which her premature labour, ten weeks early, was ascribed. It happened so suddenly that the *sage-femme* from France, whom her mother Marie de Médicis had organised to attend, never arrived. Instead, the 'poor town midwife of Greenwich' was rushed into the royal chamber, and promptly swooned from the drama of it all. She was replaced by a surgeon, and just as well, since it was a very difficult delivery. Charles constantly appeared at the bedside, emphasising that the mother's life had to be saved at all costs. And Henrietta Maria did survive. The premature baby, a boy who was hastily christened Charles-James, died the same day. A barge took his little body up-river to Westminster, where he was buried in the Abbey the same night. A superstitious soul, Henrietta Maria never returned to Greenwich to give birth to a child, and she was to have many.

Perhaps it was to help Henrietta Maria overcome the gloomy associations which Greenwich now had in her mind that the project of the Queen's House was revived. The unhappy birth had happened in May 1629. Within a few months, according to the accounts of the Paymaster of the Works, the Queen's House had become the subject of 'sondry necessary workes and Reparacons', including the construction of a new roof (of thatch, since it was temporary). It was in a happy mood that Henrietta Maria followed the progress of the building – she visited the site often – for in 1630 she gave birth to the future Charles II, at St James's Palace.

Adriaen Van Stalbemt and Jan Van Belcamp's painting does not show the Queen's House in the state we know it. They depict it as a single-storey structure (presumably this can be explained by its unfinished state), with a row of eight round-headed windows arranged either side of a big central arch. Over the arch is a triangular pediment. If this is the building that existed in 1632, Jones completely reworked it. It would not be surprising if he did. In 1617, this had been one of his earliest attempts in architecture; in the intervening years he had been busy with one great commission after another – lodgings for the Marquis of Buckingham at Whitehall Palace; rebuilding the Banqueting House at Whitehall Palace after a fire; erecting St Paul's Church, Covent Garden, and laying out the piazza

The Queen's House in 1781. In 1661–2 John Webb made the building into a square by building two further bridges over the Dover road.

in front of it. He might well have revised his ideas – or come up with new ones – while the Queen's House stood neglected. It is part of the enigma of this crucially important building, to assume pride of place in the pantheon of neo-Palladianism after its publication in Colen Campbell's *Vitruvius Britannicus* in 1715, that no elevational drawings survive to show its evolution. The catalogue of the Royal Academy's 1990 exhibition of Inigo Jones's complete architectural drawings includes a drawing (now lost) of an elevation of the north front of about 1640, by an unknown Italian draughtsman. It is the only elevation to come down from before the Restoration. It shows the Queen's House as it can still be seen: a seven-bay façade of square-headed windows, those on the ground floor set into rusticated masonry, the central window of the first floor having a balcony, a round head and a tablet above. Along the skyline runs a parapet, giving a chastely rectangular profile. Two chimneys rise above it, as they do today; the drawing also shows two turrets. These would have been little banqueting rooms, following the Elizabethan practice. In the sixteenth century there had been a vogue among country-house builders for providing rooftop eyries to which guests could repair for the last course of a meal. Roofs were important: it was common practice to walk up and down on the leads. So it must have been at the Queen's House. The lost drawing shows that this side of the building, facing the river, may have been decorated with mural paintings of trophies, sacrifices and triumphs. This suggests that the House was intended as a place to receive guests arriving by water, perhaps with theatre or poetry. Because of its position east of London, Greenwich was often the first stopping place for arriving ambassadors and other great people. There they rested until ready to make their grand entrance into the capital. In 1636 the newly arrived Spanish ambassador stayed at Greenwich incognito for more than a week, unable to appear publicly until preparations for his first official appearance, which he wished to make 'in the most pompous and magnificent manner', according to Anzolo Correr, the Venetian ambassador, had been completed. The Caroline court may well have wanted somewhere to receive such resplendent personages, incognito or not. It retained this function into the eighteenth century, long after the palace itself had disappeared and the ground between the Queen's House and the river was the site of the Seamen's Hospital. The architect Nicholas Hawksmoor, writing his *Remarks of the Founding and Carrying on the Buildings of the Royal Hospital at Greenwich* in 1727, remembers that Queen Mary wanted to add four pavilions to the Queen's House to make that 'little Palace compleat' into 'a Royal Villa for her own Retirement, or from whence Embassadors, or publick Ministers might make their Entry into London'. The Queen died in 1694 and the pavilions were never built. But the Queen's House continued to serve as a reception depot for very grand arrivals to England. On a foggy evening in September 1714, a rowing barge arrived and King George I, yet to be crowned, stepped on to English soil for the first time at Greenwich. He was taken by torchlight to the Queen's House. (Such was the excitement at the Hospital that the sculleryman was later forgiven for the loss of 40s worth of pewter pots which vanished in the commotion.) George III's bride, Princess Charlotte, would have landed at Greenwich, had not fickle September weather forced her ship to put in at Harwich. The future Queen Caroline, who was to have a close, not to say intimate, association with the area when she lived in Blackheath following her separation from the Prince of Wales, disembarked at Greenwich in 1795.

Charming, pretty, scheming, devout, frivolous, a great breeder of children and a concerned mother, Henrietta Maria had, alas, no feeling for English politics. Any intervention she made in her husband's affairs was disastrous. Charles can only have been increasingly preoccupied with the gathering storm. Yet, temperamentally averse from business of state, even he was able to detach himself from the ominous unfolding of events to a surprising degree. Together they were able to exercise their shared love of art in finishing the Queen's House. On 18 May 1635, Correr reported to the Doge and senate: 'On Wednesday his Majesty went to Greenwich with the queen. It is thought that they will both stay there at least six weeks, the king to enjoy the pleasures of the chase, and the queen to see the completion of a special erection of hers, which is already far advanced.' Two years later they once again went 'to see some buildings of the Queen at Greenwich'. By this time, 1637, most of the carving of the interior had been finished, though the year still witnessed a dispute between Inigo Jones ('Mr Surveyor') and the Commissioners of the Navy over the impressment of Thomas James and Richard Durkin. They were carvers. The Navy wanted them to adorn the *Sovereign of the Seas*, being built at Woolwich.

Chimneypieces were designed, made and installed in the late 1630s. Painters were at work too. The Tuscan artist Orazio Gentileschi, patronised by the Duke of Buckingham and installed in his Whitehall house, had lingered there after the latter's assassination, awaiting payment from the King, much to the annoyance of Buckingham's widow. Now he was at work on panels for the ceiling of the Great Hall and the cove of the ceiling of the Queen's bedroom. The theme of the Hall paintings was Peace surrounded by the Muses and the Arts, neatly combining the feminine beauty and cultural sophistication that characterised Henrietta Maria. The accounts mention carved picture frames, dispersed during the Commonwealth. There were also a large number of sculptures, according to the *Inventory* made by the Parliamentary Commissioners in 1649-50. They included Bernini's famous bust of Charles I, made from the triple portrait, showing each profile and the full face, painted by Van

Dyck. (It was a countenance 'doomed', pronounced Bernini when he saw it. 'Never have I beheld features more unfortunate.' Van Dyck also undertook a triple portrait of Henrietta Maria, and stayed at Greenwich to paint it.) The fine arts of sculpture and painting combined with the applied arts of furniture and decoration in the enrichment of this building. An item in the accounts read: 'To … Zachary Tailer Carver for carving Tenn Pedestalls of Timber for marble Statuaes to stand on with Bulls heads festons, fruites leaves & flowers att lxs the peece.' Contemporaries regarded the Queen's House, as well they might, as an exquisite production which was the best of its kind. To quote one of them, Henrietta Maria 'hath so finished and furnished, that it far surpasseth all other of that kind in England'. By the end of the century, it had become an icon, not just of taste but of the Stuart monarchy. Hence its preservation. It would have been all too natural to sweep it away as part of the grand baroque development of the Seamen's Hospital; the Queen's House was out of style and out of scale. Instead Queen Mary, herself a Stuart, insisted that it was kept as the focus of the composition.

There were only three years for the royal family to enjoy the Queen's House. It was finished in 1639. On 10 February 1642 Henrietta Maria and Charles spent a night at Greenwich for the last time. Henrietta Maria was on the way to Dover, from where she would embark with her daughter Princess Mary to Holland. The princess was engaged to William Prince of Orange. It was a sign of the low ebb of Stuart fortunes that she had made so poor a match, and was being taken out of the country when she was only ten. It was an excuse for Henrietta Maria to try to raise money for her husband on the Continent. From Greenwich, Charles went north with the Prince of Wales. In a couple of months the Civil War had begun. Henrietta Maria returned, but not to Greenwich – London was not friendly to the Royalist cause – and not to a life of gardens, art and masques. She landed in Yorkshire, and was now, as she called herself, 'Generalissima', riding at the head of the troops she had brought over. But not all the exertions of this diminutive, high-spirited, dark-eyed woman, capable of great courage in dreadful circumstances, could save her world from its fate. Just a fortnight after the birth of her last child, a daughter, in the summer of 1644, Henrietta Maria embarked from Falmouth, in Cornwall, to France. She was convinced she was dying. 'Adieu, my dear heart,' she wrote to her husband. Her ship was pursued and attacked; with its rigging damaged, it limped to the shore of Brittany, where the local people at first thought the royal party were pirates. The Queen of England, persuading them otherwise, managed to scramble ashore over the rocks, and sheltered in a thatched hut. For the next five years she could only watch, Generalissima no more, as the last act of her husband's tragedy was played out. In 1649 his composed figure stepped out of a window of Inigo Jones's Banqueting House in Whitehall on to the scaffold where the two executioners, grotesquely dressed in tight woollen clothes and false beards, awaited him.

Poor Inigo Jones had sometimes been at the King's side during the War: his architectural knowledge made him an expert on fortification. In 1645 he was among the many Royalists who sought to hold out in Basing House, in Hampshire, against a siege. He was consulted on its defence, but the garden walls could not withstand the pounding of artillery and the Roundheads poured in. They killed indiscriminately. Jones, hated for his contribution to the masques in the 'Queen's Dancing Barne', was stripped naked, and the old man had to make an unceremonious escape, wrapped in a blanket. The beheading of Charles I broke his heart, and in 1652 he died (as the architect John Webb, who married a close relation of Jones's, wrote in 'The Vindication of Stonehenge Restored') 'through grief, as is well known, for the fatal calamity of his dread master'.

I HAVE NEVER LIVED SO MERRILY AS I HAVE DONE THIS PLAGUE-TIME

Q UEEN HENRIETTA MARIA returned to England six months after the triumphant restoration of her son, Charles II, in 1660. She could not establish herself immediately at Greenwich, since it was in no state to receive her. Instead, she lodged at Whitehall Palace. But her stay there was brief. Soon she was off back to France, taking her daughter, Henrietta Anne, to be married to the Duke of Orleans, brother of Louis XIV. By the time she returned, in the summer of 1662, Greenwich had been made ready for her, and she went straight there.

The intervening years of exile – eighteen of them since her last night at the Queen's House – had told on Henrietta Maria's features. She had always been small; now she looked pinched, and she dressed always in black. To the Frenchwoman that she was, however, the colour was not unbecoming. With consummate chic she was accompanied by twenty-four menservants, in cassocks of black velvet embroidered with golden suns. She was not generally a popular figure. She was regarded as one of the causes of the Civil War and the miseries that came after it. It was perhaps in recognition of this that, in her first years back in England, she withdrew from the public gaze to Greenwich. Later she would make the building that became known as Somerset House, then called Denmark House, after Anne of Denmark, her principal home, the music from the concerts she gave there drifting out over the Thames to beguile the ears of the watermen who plied their vessels on the river.

The Greenwich to which Henrietta Maria returned was a changed place from the one she had left in 1642. London as a whole sided with Parliament during the Civil War. There were probably more Royalists in Greenwich than round the capital, if only as a result of the employment which the court gave to locally settled people, such as musicians. But they seem to have kept their heads down. The hundreds of Royalist soldiers who had been defeated by Fairfax on Blackheath found that they were hooted and pelted by the Greenwich watermen when they fled into the town. When, in the last days of the Civil War, the Earl of Norwich camped a band of Royalists in the Park in the hope to raise recruits, he had little joy of it; everyone who wanted and was able to fight for the cause had already joined up.

The proceedings of the manor court of 1645, at the height of the Civil War, suggest that, for most people, life continued much as it always had. Bakers, butchers and brickmakers were fined, as they always had been, for selling underweight goods; citizens neglected to remove muck heaps from beside stables; failed to keep their drains clean; fed their pigs on the highway 'to the grate annoyance of passers by'; persisted in keeping their boats where they should not, and then abusing 'the jurie with verie vile and uncivill language'; and would not take down structures that they had illegally erected beside the dock. These were everyday misdemeanours. Already, though, there is a hint that royal possessions were being treated with a freedom that residents would never have permitted themselves before. Richard Hewes, the seller of underweight bricks, was persistently fined for such offences as 'suffering his hoggs to goe into the King's house' and the 'erecting of cottages on the King's waste'. The waste was the land immediately outside the Park wall.

The advent of the Commonwealth signalled an end for all the *douceur de vivre* associated with the Caroline court. The glorious art collections were dispersed among government buildings, lent to ambassadors, delivered to Oliver Cromwell for his own apartments, embezzled in the confusion or straightforwardly sold. Some paintings went to the court musicians and other functionaries at Greenwich whom Charles had been unable to pay. In 1652 the diarist John Evelyn visited 'Old Jerome Laniere' who had acquired, among other pictures, an intaglio portrait of Queen Elizabeth: he had been one of her servants and said it was an excellent likeness. A couple of loyal souls seem to have bought what they could, to keep safely until the monarchy was restored.

The state apartments in the palace were turned into stables. That degradation must have been a conscious insult to the memory of the men and women who had peopled them until hostilities commenced. Later they housed prisoners from the First Dutch War, 1652–4, which broke out as a consequence of Cromwell's Navigation Act of 1651. For a time the Queen's House was made over 'by the rebels to Bulstrode Whitlock, one of their unhappy counsellors', as John Evelyn recorded in his diary. Bulstrode moved out. Then came the idea that it should be occupied by Oliver Cromwell himself. That did not come to anything, but it may have had the effect of restraining the depredations. Land from around the Park – the waste between the Park wall and the road – was sold to speculators who wanted to build on it. The priory buildings, the kitchen and the privy gardens were acquired by Uriah Babington and Thomas Griffin; Babington had been the King's barber for ten years and was owed nearly £4,000. The Fish Offices were sold, appropriately enough, to Richard Salmon. All these sales were cancelled after the return of Charles II, which meant that the new owners, if they kept their property, had to pay twice.

Crowley House, begun by the City merchant and zealous royalist, Sir Andrew Cogan, and completed by the regicide MP Gregory Clement – thrown out of Parliament, according to one account, for misbehaviour with a serving maid at Greenwich. Under Charles II, it was owned by George Bowerman, who obtained an order to ballast the King's ships, which he did from nearby Ballast Quay (it survives today). Bowerman sold it to the great Newcastle ironfounder, Sir Ambrose Crowley. The grounds were littered with anchors in the eighteenth century.

Throughout the first half of the seventeenth century, courtiers had been building themselves good houses in up-to-date styles around the Park. These also suffered a diminution. Their fate was not so bad as Placentia, since they were bought by new owners, but the shades of the Cavalier court were just as effectively banished. The land attached to Swanne House, standing on the site of what is now Greenwich Market, was divided up into ten building plots. East of the palace, the ardent Royalist Sir Andrew Cogan had built the house that, in the next century, became known as Crowley House, after its then owners (its site is now occupied by the generating station). It had not even been finished at the outbreak of the Civil War, but is reputed to have cost a fortune; Gregory Clement, the Parliamentarian, bought it for £832, supposedly less than a fifth of what Sir Andrew had spent in erecting it. Unabashed by his role as a regicide, Clement shrewdly acquired a pair of stoves from the palace kitchens to help complete it; they were emblazoned with the royal arms. At the Restoration, stoves or no stoves, he was beheaded. Wricklemarsh House, on the other side of Blackheath, had always been home to a Parliamentarian, and so it remained. Its owner, Colonel Thomas Blount, had been one of the two men in Kent whom Charles I refused to pardon in 1642. He relished the military life, to the extent of organising a mock battle between Parliamentarians and Royalists on Blackheath. When John Evelyn was robbed at a place called Procession Oak outside Bromley in 1652, Blount used his magistrate's powers to send out a hue and cry in pursuit of the two cut-throats (though it was as a result of Evelyn's having notices of the theft distributed around London shops by an officer of the Goldsmiths' Company that his property was recovered).

'A very stately seat for situation and brave plantations,' is how Samuel Pepys found the Hall, marvelling at 'a Vineyard, the first that ever I did see'. It was typical of Blount. Like so many of Pepys's acquaintance, he had an inquisitive, inventive mind. But the wine was 'good for little', according to Evelyn. Hardly surprising: the description of the soil given by Sir Thomas Hanmer in his *Garden Book*, which 'naturally grows nothing but ling and furze', does not sound very promising. 'The Colonell sayth hee uses no dung nor compost to this barren earth of his vineyard, which is very strange.'

Gone were the fabulous masques and elegant fashions. The tone of life during the Commonwealth can be judged from the kill-joy rules that Greenwich residents, like everyone else, laboured under and sometimes infringed. They incurred fines for the keeping of ninepins, swearing and going to an ale-house at a time when the culprit should have been at church.

As for Placentia, the palace was a wreck. It was worse treeated than any of the other major palaces. Besides, it was old and nothing had been done to maintain it for twenty years. When the King came to inspect the palace at Greenwich in 1661, the gates had to be broken open to enter the park.

In name, Greenwich still belonged to Henrietta Maria, but that did not prevent Charles II from having ideas for it. As an exile, he had been exposed to the bronzing effect of the Sun King: he had seen how things could be done. He had a natural inclination to architecture, too. What he did not have was much money. But the plans he laid for Greenwich were on the grandest of scales. Just as it had suffered most during the Commonwealth, so now it was the subject of Charles II's most ambitious building project. Within a year of his return he had formed the idea of sweeping away the mouldering buildings by the river and replacing them with a new palace. Like so many previous occupants of Placentia, Charles II was entranced by this magnificent site. He had a great affinity for ships, and would have enjoyed the sights of the river.

In October 1661 John Evelyn discussed the site of the new palace with Sir John Denham, the Surveyor of Works. Evelyn's idea was to set it back from the river frontage, making in front of it 'a large Square Cutt' which would 'let in the Thames like a Baye'. A handsome conception, but even in Charles's imagination it must have seemed too expensive to be built. But he was fixed in his intention of 'quite demolishing the old' palace, as the King himself told Evelyn in January the next year. A model for the replacement palace seems to have been in existence. It may or may not have been by Inigo Jones's hagiographer and relation by marriage, John Webb (of Butleigh, Somerset). But it was certainly Webb who designed the one range that was actually built in 1664.

In the meantime Charles had to make ready the Queen's House for his mother's arrival. The Tudor palace was too far gone to save, and most of it came down in the course of 1662. For a time, an apartment was retained for the Earl of St Albans, Henrietta Maria's devoted major domo (said to be her lover or even husband) who was granted the custody of the palace. But these lodgings did not survive long, and in a few years everything except the chapel, now used as a storehouse, had been swept away. For the Queen's House this had the advantage of opening up its view of the river, previously blocked by the old buildings.

It was felt that the Queen's House could be made comfortable – if only its two halves either side of the road could be united. Inigo Jones had conceived the building as a caprice, the backdrop for reception ceremonies, a little palace of art and a grandstand from which to view diversions. He did not think of it as a dwelling house. To convert it into one, the hollows of the H-plan were filled in, at first-floor level, by building new rooms at either end, supported on bridges. This work provided two suites of state-rooms on the first floor, all at the same level. Two suites? Clearly

Charles did not expect his mother to stay in residence for ever; perhaps he had not expected her to return there at all. His interest in Greenwich began shortly after his marriage, and part of the object in rearranging the Queen's House was to provide matching apartments that formed a King's Side (on the east) and Queen's Side (on the west). The architect responsible was probably Webb, whose additions were so sympathetic to the original as to be virtually identical in style. Fortunately the proposal to erect corner pavilions, which would have destroyed the purity of the façades, never got beyond the digging of foundations in 1663.

Landscape gardening, on a scale appropriate to Charles II's proposed new palace, had already begun. By April 1662 the hill below Duke Humphrey's Tower had been transformed into a series of terraces or Giant's Steps. The diarist Samuel Pepys described the effect as 'very magnificent'. It is no wonder that these garden works should have impressed him: they were a novelty for Britain. In France Charles II and his mother had seen the works of André Le Nôtre, who had laid out Versailles for Louis XIV. That great man was consulted, and even prepared plans. Who carried them out is not known; inevitably the work executed was done to a reduced scale.

The trees which Pepys saw may have been the first ever to have been planted in this country for visual effect. In the French manner, they were marshalled into avenues, striding out over the landscape as straight as a surveyor could make them. These avenues suited the French style of hunting, not that this was what Charles had in mind; he had not inherited his grandfather James I's passion for the chase. They required a large number of young trees: six thousand elms were planted in 1664. The elms have gone, of course, but a considerable number of the gnarled Spanish chestnuts of this era survive. So do the ruins of his avenues, impressive in their way, though they would have been far more so if the site had been level. Then, for example, Blackheath Avenue would have ended in a splendid vista of the Queen's House and later the Royal Naval College (as Charles II intended it, his palace) beyond it. Instead it ended, so to speak, in mid-air, a statue of Major-General James Wolfe of Quebec being raised in 1930 (a gift from the Canadian people) as its terminal feature. There is a theory that Le Nôtre was never told that the site was not level.

The palace itself was designed by John Webb. Originally it was to have been three ranges, enclosing a big open courtyard giving on to the river; the southern block would have been crowned by a dome. Then came a scheme to make the centrepiece the Queen's House, enlarged and domed. In the event only one range – the Charles II Wing of the Seamen's Hospital – was constructed. It is in a heavier style than the great Inigo would have favoured. The length of the block is emphasised by the masonry; in deliberate contrast to this, columns in the centre and pilasters at the end rise up through the full height of the building to the cornice. There is a centrepiece with a pediment; but again, the ends are emphasised by attic storeys in which the vertical thrust of the pilasters is continued. These tensions justify the claim that this is a Baroque building – the first in England.

When Parliament had invited Charles to take the throne, they had sent him a chest containing £50,000 for his personal needs; the sight of so many golden coins, after years of frustration and poverty in exile, made him laugh out loud. But the cornucopia of the royal finances was by no means infinite, and by the end of the 1660s Charles was forced to concede that he would never realise his vision of a new waterside palace. Perhaps it was as well for him: the country might not have appreciated such an emphatic display of absolutism.

Webb died in 1672. The previous year he described himself, in a new version of his *Historical Essay on the Origins of the Chinese Language*, as 'very fairly at leisure, until his Majesty shall bee gratiously pleased to proceed towards the perfecting of his new Royall Palace at Greenwich; the designing and ordering whereof comanded formerly my cheifest time'. (The *Historical Essay* shows how far Webb shared the inquisitiveness of his times; it was a brave venture, since he never visited China nor learnt to read Chinese.) Admirers of English architecture must be grateful that not more was completed, leaving the field relatively clear for the altogether greater geniuses of Wren and Hawksmoor, architects of the Royal Naval Hospital. Still, as Pepys recorded in July 1665, the King was 'mightily pleased with his new buildings'. Later Wren's son, also Christopher, was generous enough to call it 'a graceful *Pavilion*'. And the new range was soon put to good use – not as a resplendent setting for monarchy, but as temporary offices for naval administration during the Great Plague of 1665.

* * *

Thus it was in Greenwich that, from August 1665 till January 1666, Samuel Pepys had his office. He knew Greenwich already. Official business was always drawing him to the yards at Woolwich and Deptford, where he inspected rope, timber and canvas, poked into stores, investigated fire risks and organised contracts, leases and surveys. Also at Deptford lived the mistress whom he invariably refers to as 'Bagwell's wife', William Bagwell being a ship's carpenter for whom he obtained 'preferment': Pepys never scrupled to use his powers of patronage to his own sexual advantage.

To Pepys it was only a short walk from Deptford and Woolwich to Greenwich, or vice-versa. Sometimes he had a specific reason for going, when a warship was moored there, or more often one of the King's yachts. But it seems that he also simply enjoyed the walk. In the spring of 1663 he found it 'very pleasant along the green corne and peas'. Once (on 22 April 1664) he rose at four a.m., left his home in Seething Lane, went to Greenwich by river and, in the cool and mist of the early morning, 'walked with great pleasure to Woolwich, in my way staying several times to listen to the nightingales'. It was not always free from adventure. At night, he would be sure to have some stout fellow go with him carrying a blazing link or a lantern. Walking to Greenwich after having inspected the *Royal James*, in May 1663, 'I was set upon by a great dog, who got hold of my garters and might have done me hurt; but Lord, to see in what a maze I was, that having a sword about me, I never thought of it or had the heart to make use of it, but might for want of that courage have been worried.'

Pepys and his contemporaries, like the Cavaliers of an earlier generation, viewed Greenwich as a place of resort. It was somewhere to go for an outing. 'Away back home,' he writes in May 1665; 'and not being fit for business, I took my wife and Mercer down by water to Greenwich at 8 at night, it being very fine and cool, and moonshine afterward – mighty pleasant passage it was. There eat a cake or two, and so home by 10 or 11 at night, and then to bed.' He spent a happy summer afternoon in 1662, visiting Greenwich to see the King's yacht, the palace and the Park. Afterwards he went to one of the taverns that had a reputation for music.

It is a sign of Greenwich's gentility that Pepys had friends round about. Foremost among them, and typical of the salty character of the area, was Captain Cocke, a hemp merchant who served as Commissioner for the Sick and Wounded and Prisoners of War in 1664–7. Since hemp was a naval necessity, and Pepys responsible for procuring it, they inevitably saw much of each other; he was also good company, though boisterous. His house stood next to the mansion built by Sir Andrew Cogan, on the east side of Greenwich: Pepys describes it as 'a most pleasant seat, and neat'. Then there was the lawyer Mark Cottle, Registrar of the

Prerogative Court, 'with a very pretty house, and a fine Turret at top, with windeing stairs, and the finest prospect I know about all Greenwich, save the top of the hill – and yet in some respects better than that'. It was called the Belvedere.

At Wricklemarsh House, the Colonel Blount whose hue and cry had been despatched after Evelyn's robbers, was a member of the Royal Society: that august body of scientists and scientifically inclined gentlemen – the 'college of virtuosoes' – of which Pepys himself would become President. There was much wondering at the ingenuity (and about the practicability) of Blount's 'Way-Wiser', a kind of odometer, and a new type of coach springs, which a committee of the Royal Society tried on Blackheath. 'It is very fine and likely to take,' wrote Pepys, perhaps optimistically. The Royal Society returned to Colonel Blount the next year, considering a new type of 'chariot' in which 'the coachman sits astride upon a pole over the horse, but does not touch the horse, which is a pretty odde thing; but it seems it is more easy for the horse, and, as they say, for the man also'.

A walk to Deptford brought Pepys to that other diarist, John Evelyn, the greatest connoisseur of his age. Evelyn had moved to his wife's property of Sayes Court, Deptford, in 1652. There he created an elaborate garden out of what had previously been 'a rude orchard, and all the rest one entire field of 100 acres, without any hedge'. He lovingly planted walks, groves, enclosures and plantations, his pains being rewarded, after the Restoration, by visits from both the Queen Mother, Henrietta Maria, and King Charles II. Like all gardeners, Evelyn was at the mercy of the winter weather. In January 1684, when the Thames froze over, he went to Sayes Court to find 'the oranges and myrtles very sick, the rosemary and laurels dead to all appearance, but the cypress likely to endure it'. These comments come from the famous diary that was discovered in an old clothes basket at his brother's house at Wotton in 1817.

The weather was not the only danger Sayes Court was to contend with. In February 1698, Deptford was graced, if that is the word, by the presence of the Emperor of Russia, Peter the Great. He came to England to study shipbuilding, and after some time visiting the sights of London, withdrew to John Evelyn's house. For four and a half decades, Evelyn had studied to make the house and its garden a reflection of his antiquarian learning and discriminating taste. These qualities seem to have been lost on Peter. His researches into shipbuilding were accompanied by dissipation and vandalism. He and his entourage ('right nasty,' according to Evelyn's bailiff) slept anywhere, at any hour. After Peter had left, Evelyn had Sir Christopher Wren and the King's gardener, George London, value the damage. They found that doors had been taken down and burnt, three hundred window panes had been smashed, the Dutch tiles in the fireplaces needed replacing, floors were 'dammag'd by Grease and Inck', and every piece of fabric in the house – curtains, counterpanes, bedhangings, tapestries – had been torn and soiled. The paintings were riddled with bulletholes. Outside, all the lawns had been pitted with holes 'by their leaping and shewing tricks upon it'. A particular entertainment had been for the Russians to push each other through the hedges on wheelbarrows. It was judged that the depredations amounted to the large sum of £350.

The Lords of the Treasury reimbursed Evelyn and his tenant Admiral Benbow without demur. William III was so pleased that England had received Peter as a guest that he commissioned Sir Godfrey Kneller to paint his portrait. Peter's return present was a big uncut diamond, wrapped, characteristically, in a piece of dirty paper.

During the Plague year, Pepys applied himself to making ready the King's ships for the Second Dutch War of 1665–7. But it was not all work. Prime among his distractions at Greenwich was Mrs

Pennington. Pepys had a taste for modest and seemingly virtuous women, and felt it 'very strange' that this daughter of a knighted alderman did not, after a short acquaintance, repel the hand he put inside her chemise to feel her breasts. She was, however, exceedingly taken with the contemporary fashion for déshabillé, as portrayed in the paintings of Lely. She must have been proud of her charms. Another time, a barrel of oysters inspired further ardours, though, as with other of Pepys's adventures, he seems to have had to content himself with groping. His hopes must have been high when, having been 'mighty merry and free' with her during supper from the King's Head tavern, he persuaded her to change into her nightgown, à la Lely. He said he would walk up and down while she was changing, his steps taking him along the walled road that crossed the Park. By the time he returned she had gone to bed, much to his chagrin.

For all such adventures, these were grim times. Pepys, humane as well as all too human, pitied 'the horrible Crowd and lamentable moaning of the poor seamen that lie starving in the streets for lack of money – which doth trouble and perplex me to the heart'. The wretched condition of people on the Kent Road also moved him. Further, for all the consolations provided by Mrs Pennington and others, the removal to Greenwich was a cost that Pepys would rather not have borne. His wife and household were still living at Woolwich, while a maid kept the London house going. Pepys was not the only person seeking to escape the Plague, and his landlady got a good price for her lodgings. But it had to be done. When Pepys went to the City, he was relieved and surprised when he found shopkeepers, including pretty ones, still on their feet. Like everyone else, he could only watch powerlessly as the Bill of Mortality rose to over a thousand a week. One day when he walked from Woolwich to Greenwich in August 1665, he saw

a coffin with a dead body therein, dead of the plague, lying
in an open close belonging to Coome farme, which was
carried out last night and the parish hath not appointed
anybody to bury it – but only set a watch there day and
night, that nobody should go thither or come thence,
which is a most cruel thing – this disease making us more
cruel to one another then we are [to] dogs.

It was not until the end of the year that the Plague had 'abated
almost to nothing', and he could look forward to a return to
Seething Lane. This happy event took place on 22 January 1666.

Still, he had to conclude, on 21 December 1665, 'I have never
lived so merrily . . . as I have done this plague-time.' In 1669 he
gave Greenwich the accolade of being 'a very pretty place'.

* * *

One of the books in Pepys's library is said to have been Sir Jonas
Moore's survey of the entire length of the Thames. Moore was
another of the ingenious figures in Pepys's acquaintance. Very tall,
very fat, with grey eyes and the fat man's delicate skin, he cannot
have been easily overlooked. Trained as a mathematician, he was
also expert in draining the Fens, cartography and fortification.
John Aubrey, in his *Brief Lives*, concluded that he 'was one of the
most accomplisht Gentlemen of his time; a good Mathematician,
and a good Fellowe'. In short, he was the sort of man whom
Pepys might be expected to like.

Moore never lived at Greenwich, but he was to make a power-
ful contribution to its history. For he was not only a mathematician and surveyor, he was also an astronomer. It is no wonder
that, given his bent, he should have taken study of the heavens
into his repertoire. This was an area in which even amateurs could
still make a contribution to knowledge, and it also had a highly

Effigies Ionæ Moore Matheseos Professoris Ætat: suæ 45 An: Dm: 1660

Sir Jonas Moore, the mathematician, discussed his duodecimal system of mathematics and the concept of time in the Old Testament with Samuel Pepys. He was the prime mover behind founding the Royal Observatory.

valuable application. The anxiety that Pepys experienced over trade with Tangier (he was secretary to the Commmission that ran this newly acquired colony) is evidence of the rudimentary state of navigation at sea. Sometimes even the most experienced seamen steered by a combination of intuition and guesswork. Ships that were far from their supposed position on the charts could be wrecked, or fall into enemy hands. As trade by sea expanded and the number of colonies grew, the security of English shipping became a rising concern. Eventually, in 1714, Parliament itself took action by proposing the enormous prize of £20,000 to the person who established a means of calculating longitude at sea. Forty or so years earlier, Charles II had made his own contribution by establishing the Royal Observatory at Greenwich. The prime mover in this work had been Sir Jonas Moore.

It was the sort of project that would have appealed to one aspect of the King's nature. He shared with so many men of his age a fascination with science. He brought a professional from France to create a laboratory at St James's Palace, and had his own 'elaboratory' filled with 'chymical glasses' at Whitehall, where he conducted experiments. Even so, constitutionally averse from anything that would cause him trouble, he might not have got round to founding the Royal Observatory had his interest in science not been reinforced by another predilection – the great weakness to which all the others in his personality were subsumed – his appetite for women.

In 1674, the first woman in his affections was Louise de Keroualle, the voluptuous Breton beauty whom he created Duchess of Portsmouth. She had first made an impression accompanying Charles's sister, Henrietta, Duchess of Orleans, on a visit to the English court. She was later sent back by Louis XIV, to promote what would later have been called an entente cordiale between England and France. It was her mission to meddle in politics, and meddle she did – not only in politics, but any matter where a countryman's interests were affected. To that end she took up the cause of a 'bold and indigent' Frenchman who called himself Le Sieur de St Pierre. He claimed to have found an easy means of discovering longitude by astronomy alone. Had this been possible, it would have been of immense benefit to mariners, since the only method by which longitude could be established involved knowing the ship's local time (easily done by observation) and comparing it to that at a 'prime meridian', which was impossible given that there was then no clock which could keep time accurately at sea. Charles II, badgered by his mistress, put the matter of St Pierre's claims to a Royal Commission, its seven members all drawn from the newly established Royal Society. Four of them met on 12 February 1675, taking 'Mr. Flamsteed of Darby' as their assistant. Flamsteed, a young man of twenty-eight, had been staying with his patron, Sir Jonas Moore. As Moore was also a fellow of the Royal Society, it was probably through his influence that he obtained the position. St Pierre's theories were dismissed. Even had they been true, they would have been useless without a complete chart of the movement of the heavens, which did not exist.

The warrant directs that the King's 'astronomical observator' should devote his energies 'to the rectifying the tables of the Motions of the Heavens and the places of the fixed Stars so as to find out the so-much-desired Longitude of Places'. This was, to say the least, a big job; under the circumstances, the salary of £100 a year was hardly excessive. The man appointed was Flamsteed.

An oil painting by Thomas Gibson shows Flamsteed to have had regular features, a straight nose, eyes that seem to survey the spectator coolly – disconcertingly coolly perhaps – and above all a mouth that suggests determination. From the age of fourteen, he suffered from a kind of rheumatism, supposedly the result of a cold caught while bathing. Not being able to walk to his school in Derby, he had to leave it. But the illness which cut him off from the normal youthful activities allowed him to concentrate single-mindedly, when he was well enough to concentrate at all, on his passion for astronomy. He constructed his own quadrant and made observations of the sun. In later years Flamsteed liked to recall that he pursued his studies 'under the discouragement of friends, the want of health, and all other instructors except his better genius'. Ill health may have enabled Flamsteed to develop in his chosen subject, but it also seems to have left him crabbed and over-sensitive to imagined slights. Perhaps the peculiar regime of the astronomer – observing at night, sleeping by day – exacerbated the difficult side of his character.

He was twenty-three when he made the journey to London and was there introduced to Sir Jonas Moore. Moore gave him a measuring instrument which Flamsteed calls 'Mr. Townley's curious mensurator', and obtained lenses for a telescope to fit it. With the mensurator he started making systematic observations, using a quadrant to work out the time (clocks were still a rarity in England). By this time he had entered Jesus College, Cambridge, which enabled him to become ordained as a clergyman shortly after the Royal Observatory was established. In contrast to Pepys and others who took their tone from their King, Flamsteed was pious, unimpeachable in his moral behaviour and rigidly abstemious in his habits. His task as Royal Observator was principally to observe the fixed stars and the moon's course among them.

But before that could begin, the Royal Observatory needed a home. Sir Jonas Moore favoured a site in Hyde Park; Flamsteed preferred Chelsea College, established by James I but then in ruins, which had been presented to the Royal Society in 1667. The idea of Greenwich came from Sir Christopher Wren. Wren's involvement should occasion no surprise. Though he is principally remembered as the architect of St Paul's Cathedral and some fifty-two City churches, as well as the bones of the Seamen's Hospital at Greenwich, he began his career as a scientist. As the fellow of an Oxford college, Wren had moved in the circle of scientific scholars who would found the Royal Society. Many subjects, including anatomy, stimulated his intellect, but astronomy took pride of place. It was to be his principal occupation until most of his energies were absorbed by the cascade of architectural work that fell upon him, as Surveyor of King's Works, after the Great Fire of London in 1666.

Quite why he proposed Greenwich Park as the best place to build an observatory is unclear; he may well have thought that the skies above Greenwich would be clearer than those over London itself. There was already so much smoke from brewers, dyers, soap-boilers and lime-burners, as well as domestic hearths, hanging over London that in 1661 John Evelyn published proposals to remedy matters called *Fumifugium, or the Inconvenience of the Air and Smoke of London dissipated*. He may have thought the problem would get worse over time, and he would have been right. When Evelyn's work was republished in 1772, the editor, Samuel Pegge, lamented that 'since his time we have a GREAT INCREASE of Glass-Houses, Founderies and Sugar bakers to add to the black catalogue'. Foggy weather was the bane of English astronomers as it was: they did not need to contend with a smoke haze as well. Wren himself was to be the architect of the new building. There is no record of his visiting the site during its construction, however. In the context of his other commissions, it was small beer.

It would seem that Duke Humphrey's Tower had been demolished or was at least in ruins by the time it was decided to build the Royal Observatory where it had stood. During the Civil War, the Tower acquired yet another new name: Greenwich Castle. It was still standing when Jonas Moore drew that survey of the Thames, of which Pepys owned a copy, in 1662. But the royal warrant authorising construction talks of 'the highest ground at or near the Place where the Castle stood', so presumably it was no longer there. The foundations remained, however, and for the sake of economy it was decided to re-use them. 'Provided that the whole sum to be expended and paid shall not exceed £500,' states the warrant emphatically: economy was the keynote of the whole Observatory project. The money to fund the building work came from the sale of decayed gunpowder, which was then reconditioned and, oddly, sold back to the ordnance.

On 27 July 1675 that far-ranging and inventive scientist Robert Hooke (like Wren, also an architect) records in his diary: 'To Greenwich. Set out Observatory. Saw Flamsteed's level. Dined at Nightingales in the Park ...' The foundation stone was laid on 10 August at 3.14 p.m., with Flamsteed casting a mock horoscope for the birth of the new building. By Christmas it had been roofed. In May 1676 Flamsteed reported that everything except the Sextant and Quadrant Houses – separate structures that stood in the little garden – had been completed. Flamsteed moved into the Observatory later that month before a partial eclipse of the sun.

'We built indeed an Observatory at Greenwich not unlike what your Tower will prove,' wrote Wren to Bishop Fell some years later (referring to the proposed new Tom Tower at Oxford); 'it was for the Observator's habitation and a little for pomp.' For pomp, Wren made the most of the need to create an observation room with very tall windows; he did so in the form of a tower, appearing flat from the front but octagonal within, which gave the Observatory a faintly castle-like appearance – perhaps recalling the building that had preceded it. There are little turrets at the top, for servants' bedrooms, and to either side of the façade facing the palace, Wren applied the curly scrolls called volutes. About half a dozen years later, he gave a little further dignity to this elevation by adding garden pavilions at the corners of the courtyard in front of it. The principal material was red brick – once more enjoying the vogue it had known under the Tudors. But it was a sign of the extreme economy with which the 'pomp' had to be affected that the dressings which appear to be stone are nothing more than painted wood. The bricks had been left over from the building of Tilbury fort.

This was a building to make its effect from a distance: more or less an eye-catcher in the royal Park. This is evident from the position of the front door, tucked away at the side of the main façade: not an entrance to make a grand impression on anyone actually visiting the building. It gave onto a hall on the ground floor, around which were the bedroom, drawing room and dining room of what, in effect, was Flamsteed's one-bedroom flat. Stairs lead up to the justly named Great Room, one of the few Wren interiors to survive in its original condition. The dignity and calm of Wren's architecture seem very conducive to studying the silent mysteries of the night sky. The universe which Flamsteed was observing – soon to be interpreted by Newton – seemed as ordered and mathematically inspired as the canons of classicism. Francis Place made a book of engravings of the Observatory for Jonas Moore, in which plate IX is titled *Prospectus intra Camera Stellatam* ('View within the Star Chamber'). A glance at it shows why the great height was needed. The only means by which the

PROSPECTUS INTRA CAMERAM STELLATAM

The Octagon Room in the Royal Observatory in 1676. Since the
Observatory was built on the foundations of the demolished castle, it

was not aligned on the meridian. Consequently most observations of the heavens were made from a specially constructed shed in the garden.

secrets of the heavens could be unlocked was the telescope. The longer the telescope, the more detail that could be seen. Place shows the ladder and stand necessary to support Flamsteed's eight-and-a-half-foot telescope, which had to be tilted at any angle he wished. To know the precise time at which observations were made was critically important. Consequently, two clocks by Thomas Tompion were fitted into the wall (they seem always to have been a pair, though Place shows three); they were regulated by thirteen-foot pendulums that, unusually, were hung above, rather than below, the clock faces. This reflects the ingenuity of the great Tompion.

One might almost have thought that Flamsteed was spoiled for the variety of spaces and devices available to him for observation. One of the garden pavilions formed a *Domus Obscurata*, or darkened house, for receiving sunspots and solar eclipses. There were outbuildings for large sextants, a great quadrant fixed to a wall aligned on the meridian, a sixty-foot telescope suspended from a mast, and a telescope sunk in a well. These were really the working side of the establishment. As Wren would write to Bishop Fell: 'It is the instruments in the Court after the manner I have described which are used, the roome keeps the Clocks and the Instruments that are layed by.' But none of it made Flamsteed a happy man. His private accommodation was cramped – all the more galling in view of the splendid, if little used, octagon above him.

He was provided with an idiot of an official assistant, as a result of which he had to employ another at his own expense; and he was expected to teach two pupils from Christ's Hospital as part of the bargain. He could only make ends meet by taking private pupils as well. From the beginning he was 'much troubled' (as he wrote to Towneley as early as 3 July 1675) 'with Mr Hooke', who 'will needs force his ill contrived devices on us'. These were instruments which Hooke (an authority on microscopes more than telescopes) persuaded Flamsteed to accept, but which had to be replaced later. The worst of it was that he made no allowance for the very expensive equipment without which any observatory would not be worth the name. Not that this was quite all of it. Flamsteed, locked up with his charts and his telescopes, isolated by illness as well as temperament, was a pioneer in the assembly of data; but it was not for him to make sense of it. That fell to his friend, as he originally was, Isaac Newton. Flamsteed said that Newton worked with the ore he had dug. 'If he dug the ore,' Sir Isaac said when he heard it, 'I made the gold ring.'

Newton and his contemporaries saw Flamsteed's observations as vitally important material upon which their own theories about the universe could be developed. To begin with, Flamsteed shared his data willingly with fellow scientists. But Newton's exhortations to publish at least the material that related to the major stars had the opposite effect to that intended. Flamsteed had a grander scheme; he wanted to wait until he was ready; he became secretive. He also became suspicious to the extent almost of paranoia. His *Historia Coelestis* did not appear until 1712, and then it was under the editorship of Edmond Halley, of comet fame (whom Flamsteed called a 'lazy and malicious thief').

In the history of science, the Royal Observatory was of incalculable benefit to the development of astronomy. For Greenwich, it is worth noting that it quickly became one of the wonders of England, and helped attract admiring interest in the location through the number of educated tourists drawn thither. It was not only the Royal Observatory which attracted them, of course: the Seamen's Hospital, to be described in the next chapter, was also regarded as one of the sights of Europe.

View of the Royal Observatory from the bottom of the Giant's Steps. The two summerhouses to either side of the central building appear to have been an afterthought by architect Sir Christopher Wren.

FACIES SPEC

SEPTEN:

LAST LIGHT ON THE WAVE OF TIME

Oh, heavy are the sorrows that beset
Old age! and hard it is – hard to forget
The sunshine of our youth, our manhood's pride!
But here, O aged men! ye may abide
Secure, and see the last light on the wave
Of Time, which wafts you silent to your grave;
Like the calme evening ray, that smiles serene
Upon the tranquile Thames, and cheers the sinking scene.

William Lisle Bowles, 1762–1850

IN 1672 THE SEEMINGLY interminable quarrel between the English and the Dutch was persisting, and the Duke of York, the future James II, was the Lord High Admiral in command of the English fleet. Like his brother Charles II, he had always enjoyed being around ships. But neither of them had any great aptitude for naval strategy. James proved a brave rather than brilliant Lord High Admiral. When the morning of 7 June dawned, a fleet of English and French ships was lying in Southwold Bay, off the coast of East Anglia. This force was surprised by an Admiral, Michiel de Ruyter, who, like other Dutch commanders, really did know his business. The battle that followed inflicted terrible casualties on both sides. The Dutch got the better of it. The English position was so bad that the Duke of York had to abandon two successive flagships, the *Prince* and the *St Michael*. By the end of the day there were thousands of English dead. Among the bodies floating in the water was that of Pepys's patron

Lord Sandwich, recognised only because of the Garter insignia that he had been wearing. Afterwards, the scenes in Margate, after the allied squadrons had put into shore, were appalling. The Duke of York may have been a deficient King and an indifferent commander, but he was not inhumane. The dreadful sights that confronted him made an indelible impression. He resolved to do something for the sailors who ventured so much on England's behalf.

That James II deserves credit for the idea of a Seamen's Hospital is indicated by a letter which the now elderly Samuel Pepys wrote to John Evelyn in November 1694, referring to the deposed King as 'my unhappy Master'. James had done nothing to further it during the three years he occupied the throne. But the events that followed his leaving it in 1688, when he fled to France, revived the project in the mind of his tender-hearted daughter, Queen Mary II.

England, now ruled by Mary and her Dutch husband William III, was at war again, this time forming an alliance with its former foe, Holland, against the forces of its former ally, France. The human cost was, as usual, dreadful. King William III, with whom Mary shared the throne, was away fighting in the Low Countries. It was therefore left to Mary to do what she could to relieve the suffering of the wounded of the fleet now returned to Portsmouth. In the early hours of 21 May 1692, a messenger came galloping up to London with the news of the victory. While London celebrated, the practically-minded Queen assembled fifty surgeons from the hospitals there and despatched them to Portsmouth, along with £30,000 in bounty to be distributed among the crews. She also had her Secretary of State, Lord Nottingham, bestir the Treasury 'to hasten ... the grant of Greenwich as a hospital for Seamen, which is now depending before you'.

In the end, the Hospital would be Queen Mary's memorial. She could probably not have achieved it during her lifetime. William III was a soldier, without James II's personal involvement in naval life.

The project would almost certainly have struck him as impossibly grandiose, at a time when he desperately needed money to pursue his resistance to the expansionist ambitions of Louis XIV. But the Queen's sudden death from smallpox in December 1694 opened his heart towards what had been 'the darling object of her life'. She had been popular with the English people; he, on the other hand, was not much loved. Maybe he hoped that a little of her aura would rub off on him. In any case, he could spare the palace at Greenwich better than other monarchs: being asthmatic, he could not live anywhere so watery. The charter to found a Hospital 'for the reliefe and support of Seamen serving on board the Shipps and Vessells belonging to the Navy Royall' was issued in the names of both William and Mary, and backdated to 25 October, before the Queen's death. Throughout its history the palace of Greenwich had been associated with Queens of England, often being given to them as a token of their husband's affection. Now the King's warmth towards Mary – rather greater than that of some previous monarchs towards their Queens – would be permanently embodied in the institution that was to rise on the site of the previous building.

To give the site showed generosity. And William also subscribed £2,000 towards building the Hospital 'as a further instance of Our Princely Zeal for advancing the Designe'. It was all too typical of the grandees who promised money for the project that this was slow to materialise. Hard evidence of the 'Princely Zeal' only arrived after building work had begun, in the summer of 1697. And then it did not take the form of cash, but of 'Malt Tickets', or credit vouchers against the tax on malt which the workmen would not accept at more than three-quarters of their face value. In these early years, the finances of the Hospital had to be cobbled together out of sometimes very little. Their parlous condition is at odds with the confident scale of the undertaking, planned around four handsome courts that could accommodate over two thousand veterans. The hero of the story is the man who sustained this vision through times when there was no money to realise it. In other words, the Treasurer, John Evelyn.

We encountered Evelyn in the last chapter, as Pepys's erudite friend, creating his garden, pursuing his scientific interests and writing his books at Sayes Court. Now he was an old man – seventy-four when he was appointed Treasurer of the Hospital in February 1694. Evelyn, despite his age, still had the energy necessary to pursue the project. It was one to which he had been committed for many years. As long ago as 1664, Charles II had appointed him to be one of three Commissioners for the Sick and Wounded and Prisoners of War, his area of responsibility being Sussex and Kent. Like Pepys, labouring in his office at the Navy Board, Evelyn took his duties seriously, and was active about them. He reserved half St Thomas's Hospital for the wounded who came from the fleet, and took over Chelsea College (to be considered as a possible site for the Royal Observatory) for Dutch prisoners. Apparently their only complaint, when Evelyn visited them, was that the bread was 'too fine'.

In 1666 he put the idea of a permanent hospital for the sick and wounded to Charles II, but there was no money to pursue it. Fifteen years later, though, the project was revived by Evelyn's acquaintance, the philanthropist Sir Stephen Fox. Fox was Paymaster of the Forces; the office had, of course, made him extremely rich. He proposed that Chelsea College should be purchased from the Royal Society and converted into a hospital for four hundred soldiers. From the start, it was intended that this should not only cure the wounded but look after those who were too old or disabled to find further employment. As Evelyn recorded, they were 'to be as in a college or monastery'. At a time of such Anglo-French rivalry, the fact that Louis XIV had already built Les Invalides in Paris must have encouraged Charles II in his support of the proposal. Chelsea Hospital took ten years to build, just a fifth of the time it took to finish the much larger project at Greenwich. Its opening in 1692 reinvigorated the idea of creating a similar institution for sailors.

Many of the subscribers who had said they would give money to the Hospital never did so. The Grand Committee of sixty who were supposed to oversee the project were so grand that they hardly ever met. The burden of raising the money fell upon the aged shoulders of the Treasurer. His probity, which, to judge from the diaries, might have been mildly irritating to his contemporaries, was remarkable in an age when Treasurerships were generally regarded as a bonanza for those who possessed them. It was common practice – indeed expected – that a Treasurer would use the money in his keeping to further his own ventures, and that was perfectly in order so long as the capital was produced for its intended use when required. Evelyn never drew the salary to which he was entitled. Further, he himself gave £1,000 to the project – half as much as the King himself. The foundation stone was laid on 30 June 1696, with John Flamsteed, the Astronomer Royal, on hand, to observe the 'punctual time by instruments'. The extent of Evelyn's difficulties can be judged by the shortfall in the accounts at the end of the first year: receipts £800, expenditure £5,000.

Evelyn (and his successors as Treasurer) raked together money from wherever they could, their reach sometimes extending in unlikely directions. There was already a charitable fund for seamen called the Chatham Chest, built up from the sixpence a month that had been deducted from their wages each month since 1590. From 1696 another sixpence was taken for the Hospital (the Chatham Chest finally became amalgamated with the Hospital in 1814). Fines on French merchants who had been caught smuggling, about £10,500, were made over in 1697. Early in the next century,

Captain William Kidd was brought to the scaffold for having killed a man (he struck him, according to the meticulously detailed indictment, 'with a certain wooden bucket bound with iron hoops of the value of eightpence') while on a ship called the *Adventure Galley*. It was a token charge; Kidd was a notorious pirate. His property was confiscated and given to the Hospital, contributing about £6,500. In 1700 Lord Romney, then Ranger of the Park, ceded to the Hospital his right to establish a market in Greenwich: not an overwhelmingly attractive proposition, since it was over thirty years before the Directors of the Hospital did anything about it. A lottery was also staged, exceptionally, at a time when they were otherwise banned. In 1707 the Hospital was granted all the naval prize money from captured enemy vessels which went unclaimed; this was to provide a good income in the course of the next century, with its almost incessant fighting at sea. Rather more dependable was the solid £6,000 a year which Parliament provided from the revenues of the coal tax.

It says something about the gentlemen of substance who lived around Greenwich during the eighteenth century that one of their number, Robert Osboldston, left a bequest of £20,000 to the Hospital in 1714. Like many Greenwich figures, Osboldston derived his fortune from the sea, and he was an enterprising man, having built the North and South Foreland lighthouses. The Hospital also received the income of the dues collected from ships passing these lighthouses, worth £1,400 a year. From 1729 until the Hospital was finally completed in 1751, Parliament granted £10,000 a year towards construction. In the next century, it gave the Hospital a share of the Royal Navy's income from the practice of carrying gold and jewels for merchants.

Charm, diplomacy and persistence were required to amass the funds to carry on the building work. In the early 1730s, the then Governor of the Hospital, Admiral Sir John Jennings, personally paid for the great John Rysbrack to carve a statue of George II out of a large block of marble captured from a French ship. It was hauled on to its plinth in the very centre of the Hospital on 1 March 1735. Two months later the King would have seen it when he embarked for Hanover, earmarking a new German mistress for himself and a German bride for Frederick, Prince of Wales. There it was again when he came back. Whatever its merits as sculpture, it was undoubtedly a fine piece of flattery. And it worked. Before long the King made over the estates of an attractive young Catholic nobleman, Lord Derwentwater, who had joined the Jacobite uprising of 1715. They were of enormous value to the Hospital, producing an income that rose as their mineral wealth, particularly in coal and lead, was exploited: £7,000 initially, £25,000 in 1787 and £39,000 in 1859.

On 12 August 1703, Evelyn noted another momentous event: 'The new Commission for Greenwich Hospital was sealed and opened, at which my son-in-law, Draper, was present, to whom I resigned my office of Treasurer. From August 1696, there had been expended in building £89,364. 14s. 8d.' It was a typically modest entry; without the old man's fund-raising the Hospital would probably never have come into being, though it would still be two years before it received its first pensioners. When Evelyn died in 1706, it was found that the Hospital owed him money. The first forty-two pensioners had moved into the nearly completed King Charles Court, under Captain John Clements, in June 1705.

* * *

By the time Wren inspected the site of the Seamen's Hospital, with Samuel Pepys, in the autumn of 1694, he had become the grand old man of English architecture. He must have been a formidable presence. A gentleman by birth, twice widowed, he had reached the top of two highly reputable callings, science and architecture. He had been President of the Royal Society. He had been Surveyor to the King's

Works for as much as twenty-five years. Not only had he taken the leading role in refashioning London after the Great Fire, designing its new cathedral and dozens of churches, but he had come to know all the most important figures of his time, including a succession of monarchs. Pepys, writing to Evelyn, gives Wren the credit for elevating the notion of a hospital for the wounded sailors coming from recent wars into a great and permanent national memorial: 'an *Invalides* with us for the sea, suitable in some degree to that of Paris for the land.' Something of the rather overwhelming dignity of the man is conveyed through the prose of his son, also Christopher Wren, who describes Wren's involvement at Greenwich in his filial memoir *Parentalia*:

> he Chearfully engag'd in the Work, gratis, and contriv'd the new Fabrick, extensive, durable, and magnificent, conformable to the graceful Pavilion, which had been erected there by King Charles the Second, and originally intended for his own Palace; contributing his Time, Labour, and Skill, and prosecuting the Works for several Years, with all the Expedition the Circumstances of Affairs would allow; without any Salary, Emolument or Reward (which good Example, tis to be hoped, has been since follow'd;) preferring in this, as in every other Passage of his Life, the public Service to any private Advantage of his own, by the Acquest of Wealth, of which he had always a great Contempt.

Christopher Wren junior must have known that his successor, Vanbrugh, did not scruple to take a handsome salary for his involvement, even though he made very little contribution to the design. But then Wren belonged to a different generation, a different age.

The day-to-day running of the project was delegated to Wren's lifetime Clerk of Works, Nicholas Hawksmoor. When Hawksmoor had the task, many years later, of justifying the long and costly construction to Parliament, he emphasised Queen Mary's desire for

'Magnificence'. The ear attuned to the particular music of Greenwich may hear in this an echo of Henry VIII's priorities in his development of Placentia. It was to maximise on 'Magnificence' that various other sites that had been proposed for the Hospital – Winchester Castle and elsewhere – were rejected, since they were 'both out of the way, and not frequently seen', while Greenwich was 'in the View of all the World … [a] noble Situation in the Sight of (the Grand Emporium) London'. But that was in 1727, and Hawksmoor was sensitive to criticisms that the Hospital, which had swelled somewhat in architectural conception, was too ostentatious.

No doubt Queen Mary valued the site, as her predecessors had done, for its prominence on the river, one of the first things that arriving foreigners would see. With that in mind, she did not surrender the Queen's House, which continued in use as a royal staging post on the way to London long into the eighteenth century – despite the oddity of having a royal residence in the midst of a Hospital, albeit a very imposing one. But an equal consideration was thrift. In the last chapter we saw how the one range of Charles II's palace to have been built served as offices for Pepys and his colleagues in the Navy Board during the Plague. In more recent years it had been pressed into service as a gunpowder store, and the upper windows blocked up. According to Hawksmoor, 'workmen' (presumably builders and surveyors) came from London to assess whether the King Charles Block was worth keeping.

They, as it is indifferent to all Workmen whether they get Money by destroying or erecting Fabricks, gave their Opinion that it was nothing but a Heap of Stones, and that it might lawfully and reasonably be destroyed, and turn'd into Ornaments for slight Buildings, such as the private Hotels, or the Houses commonly built by the London Workmen, often burning, and frequently tumbling down.

This advice was put to the Queen. But she insisted that it should be retained, as well as the Queen's House which did not form part of the Hospital grant. She became quite agitated about it. Or as Hawksmoor rather charmingly recounts: 'her Majesty received the Proposal of pulling down that Wing, with as much Indignation as her excellent good Temper would suffer her, order'd it should remain, and the other Side of the Royal Court made answerable to it, in a proper Time ... There was no Argument for its being taken down could prevail.' On 24 May 1695, Evelyn records: 'We made report of the state of Greenwich House, and how the standing part might be made serviceable at present for £6000.'

Furthermore, the Queen was equally emphatic that the view, or 'visto', to the river which the Queen's House had enjoyed since the demolition of the Tudor palace should also be retained.

The retention of the King Charles Block and the vista from the Queen's House determined Sir Christopher's Wren's plan. He had hoped, initially, to replace the Queen's House with an elaborate centrepiece, in the form of the chapel with a dome almost on the scale of St Paul's, around which the courts in front of it, to either side, would be constructed. This desire remained current into the era of his successor at Greenwich, John Vanbrugh. It was never effected. As a result, the focal point of the grandest parade of baroque architecture in Britain is a small, chastely rectangular house, designed as a garden caprice, an afterthought almost to the long-vanished medieval palace. There is, as the author of the Wren Society volume on Greenwich observes, 'something peculiarly English' about this outcome. Canaletto thought the Queen's House so deficient in presence that he gave it a pediment, which it never possessed, when he painted his famous view of Greenwich Hospital.

Wren built up to, and sometimes over, the boundaries of the eight-acre site. (The Hospital was always short of room to expand.) The building went on fitfully, encountering many of the difficulties to which building sites have always been subject along the way. To begin with, work on refitting the King Charles Block, in the north-east corner, raced ahead; and in the summer of 1696 the foundations of a parallel range were being dug. In February 1697, a quantity of lead was stolen, as a result of which a mastiff dog was purchased for £1 2s, with a 4s 6d collar. The Committee for the Fabrick paid a visit of inspection. They were the only sub-committee of the three constituted for the prosecution of work at Greenwich to get anything done; perhaps as a consequence, they felt they could treat themselves royally. The accounts record the bill of fare: four ribs of beef, a leg of mutton, six chickens, ten half-flasks of wine. As Clerk to the Surveyor General, Wren, Nicholas Hawksmoor was paid £20 for making architectural drawings. Early the next year, Wren was asked to submit a drawing and estimate for a hall to be added to the scheme. In the summer, the existing Clerk of Works died and Hawksmoor was appointed in his place. He was expected to live on site, his reward being 4s a day in addition to the £50 a year he received as Clerk to the Surveyor General. John James, who would design the steeple of St Alfege's Church in Greenwich in 1730, and boasted that there was 'no person pretending to Architecture among us, Sir Chr. Wren excepted, [who] has had the advantage of a better Education in the Latin, Italian and French tongues', was appointed to the seemingly unglamorous position of watchman. Soon the foundations of the Great Hall and cupola, south of the King Charles Block, were getting along, and the terrace wall had been begun.

There were difficulties over the supply of stone: so much of it being needed for St Paul's Cathedral, then also rising. The royal quarry at Portland was at full stretch. Hawksmoor was despatched to Kent, Yorkshire and elsewhere to supplement the Portland stone.

Bricks were supplied by that all-round shady individual, Daniel Defoe, best known as the author of *Robinson Crusoe*. By the end of 1699 Wren's design had been engraved, the interior of the King Charles Block was being fitted out and the terrace, or part of it, had been constructed. Then, in 1702, King William died, and Queen Anne appointed a new Commission to direct operations. (It was at this point that John Evelyn handed over the Treasurership to his son-in-law, William Draper.) The Commission included the Prince of Denmark, the Archbishop of Canterbury and other luminaries – soon to be joined by the playwright, man of fashion and now Comptroller of the Office of Works (the post immediately beneath that of Surveyor of Works), John Vanbrugh. Not that Vanbrugh had very much, if anything, to do with the design of the Hospital at this stage: later he succeeded Wren as Surveyor at Greenwich, for which he claimed the salary that Wren had nobly forgone; but by then the design was more or less fixed. Instead, Hawksmoor's name appears with increased prominence in the accounts. Poor John James was promoted from watchman to assistant to the Clerk of Works. But the labour went on slowly for want of funds. In 1707 Wren wrote to the secretary at the Hospital – who happened to be William Vanbrugh, cousin of the architect – excusing himself from attending a meeting of the Commissioners, on the grounds that it clashed with another Commissioners' meeting about St Paul's. He comments: 'The best business wherein the Commission of the Fabrick of Greenwich can employ their time is to consult of money.'

No doubt they did so, but it did not dim their optimism. That year they commissioned an eager James Thornhill, then thirty-two years old, to paint the ceiling of the Great Hall. The son of an impoverished Dorset gentleman, Thornhill set out to prove himself a home-grown alternative to the fashionable French and Italian painters who were decorating the salons and staircases of the aristocracy. He saw the Painted Hall at Greenwich as a superb opportunity to advertise his talents as a history painter, and did not seek to be paid for the labour until it was finished. (This inevitably led to a dispute over how much he deserved to be paid, the price eventually being calculated by the square yard: £3 for the ceiling, £1 for the walls.) Begun in 1708, his great allegorical scheme was the first on such a scale by a British painter and took him nineteen years to complete. Afterwards he was knighted – the first British-born painter to be so – and amassed sufficient wealth to be able to purchase the old seat of his family at Thornhill in Dorset and become a Member of Parliament.

When Vanbrugh became Surveyor in Wren's place, most matters of detail had already been referred to Hawksmoor, who now had a house in Greenwich. Vanbrugh's contribution lay elsewhere. His touch can perhaps be detected in the petition, signed by him and other directors, which was presented to Parliament in 1723:

As to the building it is a great concern to us to observe that a work so pious in design and so much tending to the reputation of the Kingdom should be now standing to the view of the world as a kind of National reproach from the imperfect figure it makes. It is seven and twenty years since the building was first begun, and notwithstanding the taking in part of King Charles' Palace which lay ready built to hand the structure is not yet two-thirds advanced, the charge whereof has already stood in about £227,000, and by estimation it will require about £150,000 more to finish it; but the work has been for some time past at a total stand for want of money.

The case could hardly have been put better.

Vanbrugh died in 1726. His place at Greenwich was taken by the neo-Palladian Colen Campbell, a Scot who had several rich and influential patrons, including Sir Robert Walpole, who was now Prime Minister. But the familiar problem returned, and the year after Campbell's appointment lack of money caused work to stop altogether. On Campbell's death in 1729 Walpole put in place his protégé Thomas Ripley. It was patronage of this kind that had enabled Ripley to rise to a position of some prominence in the eyes of his contemporaries, though not of esteem. His origins had been so poor that he is supposed to have walked to London from his native Yorkshire to seek his fortune. Once there, he seems quickly to have established himself as a carpenter, being admitted to the Carpenters' Company at the age of eighteen in 1705. These humble beginnings could not be concealed by later pretension. When in 1721 Vanbrugh saw his name in a newspaper, followed by the honorific Esquire, 'such a Laugh came upon me, I had like to Beshit my Self'. His association with Walpole had been cemented by marriage to one of his servants, and the flagrant political jobbery by which his career progressed – the summit of which was the unfortunate portico that he added to the Admiralty building in Whitehall – caused derision at the hands, and pens, of those who aligned themselves against the administration. Pope had a go, not just once but three times. The anti-Ripley passion came on him at six-yearly intervals. Thus in the *Epistle to the Earl of Burlington* of 1731:

> Heav'n visits with a taste the wealthy fool,
> And needs no rod but Ripley with a rule.

In the Imitations of Horace of 1737:
> Who builds a bridge that never drove a pile?
> (Should Ripley venture, all the world would smile).

And in the Dunciad of 1743:
> See under Ripley rise a new White-hall,
> While Jones' and Boyle's united labours fall.

In view of such an onslaught, it is satisfactory to see that Ripley's Surveyorship at Greenwich was something of a success. He may not have been much of an architect, but he was a capable organiser and businessman. In the year that he assumed the position, Parliament granted £10,000 a year for continuing the work. Hawksmoor, so loyal to Greenwich, so badly used by Ripley's appointment, resigned three years later. But nothing would now stop the progress of building. With the windfall of the Derwentwater estates, the Hospital fairly sailed forward to completion. Queen Mary's Block arose as almost a mirror to King William's, with only the east side being altered by Ripley to give more accommodation. Finally, fifty-five years after the foundation stone had been laid, the Hospital was finished. Beneath the domes, behind the columns, pilasters and porticos, moved the blue-coated figures of seventeen hundred pensioners, for whose accommodation this masterpiece of English architecture had been achieved.

* * *

'The English say that their palaces are like hospitals, and their hospitals like palaces; and the exterior of St James's and of Greenwich justifies this saying.' Ostensibly the author of these words was Don Manuel Alvarez Espriella; in reality the Don's *Letters from England*, 1807, were written by the poet Robert Southey, who sheltered behind an exotic pseudonym in order to reflect freely upon the customs of his fellow countrymen. In the case of Greenwich, though, his observation was something of a commonplace. The Hospital was quite obviously much grander than any of the palaces owned by the royal family; the contrast with the beautifully proportioned but nevertheless miniature Queen's House, which *was* a palace, only emphasised the point.

It was also regarded as one up on the French: Greenwich was thought to be at least as splendid as Les Invalides, probably more so.

Thus Valentine Green, in *A Review of the Polite Arts in France ... Compared with their Present State in England* of 1782: 'L'Hotel Royal des Invalides, at Paris, may exult in its beautiful dome, and glory in the munificence of its foundation, without hurting our feelings, while the Royal Hospital of Greenwich can vie with their Palaces in magnificence ...' 'Magnificence' again. But where did this leave the men who inhabited the Hospital? One of them was John Worley. This nonagenarian looked so venerable, with his white hair and patriarchal beard, that Thornhill made him the model for a depiction of winter on his great ceiling. He had spent seventy years at sea. Seafaring did not, however, inculcate the best drawing-room manners, and at the age of ninety-six he could still misbehave, using foul language and getting drunk. His punishment was to be 'put in the confining house for four days and each meal to be exposed on the elevated place in the hall, and to live on bread and water for a week, and to wear the badge for swearing, to lose two sennights' allowance money, and not to go out of the Hospital for one month from that date'. There was no lash; otherwise naval discipline was maintained, with naval severity.

* * *

The naval feeling was continued, more acceptably perhaps, in their dress and lodgings. The pensioners of Greenwich Hospital had a uniform before even the navy itself: first grey, then brown, finally blue. Originally the coat was accompanied by knee-breeches but these were replaced by trousers in the 1830s, during the governorship of Sir Thomas Hardy. (This was the Hardy who had been Nelson's flag-captain at Trafalgar, immortalised as the recipient of his famous dying words. By the time he became Governor of Greenwich Hospital in 1834 he was First Sea Lord and soon to become a vice-admiral.) In popular prints the pensioners are invariably depicted as peg-legged, missing arms or blind. 'Do all Englishmen have only one arm or one leg?' inquired the future Queen Caroline, with typi-cally misplaced humour, on disembarking at Greenwich in 1795. She perhaps deserved Lady Jersey's tart reply: 'No persiflage, Madame, if you please' – though the latter's asperity owed more to her position as the Prince of Wales's mistress (he had unaccountably dispatched her to meet his bride) than to sensitivity towards the gallant seamen. The wars against France had increased the numbers of *mutilés de guerre*; but there were also many destitute pensioners who were sim-ply too old or feeble to go back to sea.

The four courts of the Hospital were divided into wards that perpetuated the names of great warships and admirals. In 1700 J. How described a visit to the King Charles Court, still unfinished but nevertheless full of pensioners – 'a means,' as he observed satir-

Rigaud's view of Greenwich from Castle Hill, about 1750. Below the hill, the trees planted by Charles II are reaching maturity.

ically, 'to Encourage others hereafter to venture their Limbs in the Nations Service, to be rewarded with a Lazy Life, no Money, and short Commons'. Every pensioner was 'design'd a distinct Cabbin to himself, and was allotted a little more room than he is like to Enjoy in the Church-Yard'. For all How's mockery, he cannot conceal the fact that, by the standards of the poor of the day, Greenwich afforded a high level of privacy. Later, the principle of separate cabins was not universally maintained, and some berths were provided in small dormitories. This may not have been anathema to the inhabitants: at Chelsea Hospital a similar seventeenth-century arrangement has to this day been preserved by the general wish of the pensioners, who appreciate the sense of camaraderie that it generates. The German visitor Sophie von la Roche was favourably impressed when she visited in 1786, recording an attractive account in her diary:

Their dormitories are very pleasant: large, light and lofty, with cubicles containing glass windows on the side, where each has his own bed, small table, chair, wardrobe, tea and smoking outfit which he can lock up. No humanitarian with a philosophical turn of mind could be indifferent to the way in which they decorate their cubicles: a number of them have sea and land charts, with the voyages they have made marked out on them, or spots where storms have been overcome or battles fought, where they have lost an arm or a leg, or conquered an enemy ship, and so on; others have stuck figures of every nationality on cardboard, others of strange beasts in foreign lands, while a number have collected books in several languages with which they amuse themselves.

The corridors are wide enough to admit of eight people walking abreast. It is all beautifully panelled and the floor is covered with rugs. In the centre of each passage there stands a large fireplace around which a crowd of men were sitting; two of them had a bench in the corridor, where they sat astride, leaning up against each other at play; and beneath it was a chamber (in good old English fashion) for their mutual use, so as they should not have to leave their labours.

Everything is spotless. Each man has two white shirts weekly, and a hundred and four women are employed to do the laundry and keep the place clean.

In contrast to the men's shipshape little cabins, the Governor occupied a pavilion containing twenty-two bedrooms.

So far from being the 'short Commons' cited by How, the pensioners' diet seems remarkable for its abundance, certainly as regards meat. Every man was allowed a pound of beef or mutton (generally boiled, sometimes roast) on each of five days of the week. On the pease-pottage days of Wednesday and Friday they were given a double ration of cheese (half a pound). There was not much in the way of vegetables, and the shrinkage of cheese when it was stored caused much controversy: what would have been half a pound when it arrived at the Hospital sometimes weighed rather less by the time it was served. Still, whatever gripes the pensioners had generally seem to have concerned quality of preparation rather than quantity of supply. They were served by some of their own number who earned pocket-money by doing so. The officers ate at their own tables. The minutes of the Directors' meeting provide an interesting footnote on the history of dining habits: 'Tablecloths belonging to the Officers' Tables to be enlarged so as to be used without Napkins and more to be bought so as to be clean each day.'

Originally, there was no provision for recreation of any kind. It was not until 1828 that a library and reading-room were created. Boredom must have been one reason why pensioners – such as ancient John Worley – fell victim to the temptations of the town. Those who misbehaved were compelled to wear yellow uniforms which gave them the name of canaries.

'And for the Sustenation of the Widows and the Maintenance and Education of the Children of Seamen happening to be slain or disabled ...' So read the words of the original charter. Eventually the Hospital did employ a teacher, whose first classes seem to have been in 1715. Out of this developed a regular Hospital school. But the needs of widows were never adequately met. Some found employment in the Hospital as nurses: six of them to every hundred men. Typically, great attention was paid to the design of the uniforms, though when a stock of them arrived they were found to be too tight. (As Philip Newell comments in his history of Greenwich Hospital, 'this in itself was a testimonial to the catering'.) But in general women were scarcely more welcome within the precincts of Greenwich Hospital – welcome, that is, by the authorities who ran it – than they were on board ship. There were, for example, no wives. As a result, many pensioners preferred to take their food allowance as a cash payment, which enabled them to help support their families in the town rather than live in the Hospital itself. Eventually this practice became more and more popular, until payment replaced the residential functioning of the Hospital altogether.

In the early morning of 2 January 1779, a fire broke out at Greenwich Hospital which, according to the Annual Register, 'burnes most furiously'. The water tanks on top of the building were, as bad luck would have it, almost empty, so pensioners formed a human chain to pass buckets of water from the Thames. It was no good. 'At ten o'clock, the Chapel (the most beautiful in the kingdom), the dome on the south-east quarter of the building, and the great dining-hall, were entirely consumed.' Several of the wards were destroyed, and for a time the Painted Hall was in danger. At eleven o'clock some fire engines arrived from London. But the fire blazed until evening. 'The damage done is immense, and it will cost a very large sum to restore that part of the Hospital to its former beauty and elegance.' The chapel was rebuilt by James Stuart, known as Athenian Stuart because of his classical influences.

When the Hospital finally moved, its buildings were left empty until occupied by the Royal Naval College in 1873, filling the great spaces with young cadets from the other end of the naval age spectrum. In 1998 that in turn closed, when training for navy, army and air force was concentrated in a new Joint-Services College. The new occupants are Greenwich University (formerly the Polytechnic of East London) and the National Maritime Museum.

SIR JOHN VANBRUGH
PLAYS AT CASTLES

O NE OF THE MANY PEOPLE who crowded into the last
chapter as Greenwich Hospital was being built was John
Vanbrugh. As the Surveyor who succeeded Christopher
Wren, he did not leave much impression on the architecture of the
Hospital; but he did embellish another area of Greenwich – Maze
Hill, just to the east of the Park. He built at least five houses there,
one of them for himself. In some ways they were an idiosyncratic
ensemble. But they also represented a revolution in taste. So
remarkable were they that it is worth digressing on the subject of
Vanbrugh's early life in order to understand this contribution to
Greenwich.

Vanbrugh, nearly forty, had turned to architecture only three or
four years before being made a Director of Greenwich Hospital in
1703. His appointment is evidence of the speed with which this
dazzling man established himself as an authority on architecture and
taste. He had already had several careers. The only unsuccessful one
had been his first. The son of a Chester linen merchant, his unusual
surname reflecting the origins of his family in Flanders, the young
John Vanbrugh tried his hand at soldiering – in his case, the resort
of a twenty-two-year-old who did not have much idea of what to
do. He may have come to it by accident, having approached Lord
Huntingdon, a kinsman, to see if he would give him a job. As

Vanbrugh's biographer, Kerry Downes, observes, he can hardly have expected that the result of his request would be the offer of a commission as ensign in Huntingdon's newly formed regiment. Vanbrugh took it, but, for once, does not seem to have shone.

Vanbrugh's late twenties were spent languishing in a series of French jails, following his arrest at Calais for lack of the correct papers. France was going to war with Holland, and he appeared to bear a Dutch name. Once he was incarcerated, the French formed the opinion that he was a valuable property (those noble connections) and sought to trade him for a Frenchman imprisoned in London. But poor Vanbrugh was not, at that stage, of much interest to anyone. He was twenty-nine when he was released, having wasted four or five years behind bars. Within a few years, however, he had written a witty, worldly, to some people scandalous play called *The Relapse, or Virtue in Danger*. It was his first attempt for the theatre: he claimed to have written it in six weeks. From the moment the curtain went up on Boxing Day 1696, the London audience relished its urbane saltiness. Vanbrugh was a celebrity.

His career as an author continued, his greatest hit being his second play, *The Provok'd Wife*. His natural conviviality now had the outlet that had been denied it during his incarceration in France. In 1701 he built a house, rather miniature, in one of the grandest and most prominent locations in London: the grounds of the old Palace of Whitehall. The poet and satirist Jonathan Swift likened Vanbrugh's building to 'a Goose-pie', and it was known as Goose-pie House ever after. There is some doubt as to what exactly constituted a goose pie in the first years of the eighteenth century. The dish was probably known for its curious shape and ingredients. We can be sure that Swift meant no compliment. And Goose-pie House (long demolished) must have seemed very odd, with its recession and projection, its bold rusticated stonework in the centre contrasting with plain ashlar to either side, and its contrast of height between wings and centre block. The house was novel, baroque and, considering its small size, full of architectural content. This was the first of the three houses Vanbrugh would build for himself, the last being started seventeen years later on Maze Hill at Greenwich. The Greenwich house would be equally idiosyncratic.

Goose-pie House came only two years after Vanbrugh made his debut in architecture by ousting the establishment architect, William Talman, from the favour of Lord Carlisle, for the new house, almost a palace, he was building in Yorkshire. In Renaissance Italy, great artists sometimes became architects, without much preparation or training. But they could at least draw. For someone without any previously demonstrated artistic or craft skill to design a great architectural project such as Castle Howard – and supervise its execution – is virtually without parallel. At this stage, Vanbrugh had almost no skill as a draughtsman. His client had to be persuaded of his ideas through the construction of a wooden model. In his lampoon on the Whitehall house, written in 1706, Swift drew attention to his lack of experience:

Van's genius without Thought or Lecture
Is hugely turn'd to architecture.

Scholars have puzzled over whether this comment was literally true. Surely some 'thought or lecture' – that is to say, study of architecture – must have preceded his first essay. But no: there is no evidence of his having worked with an architect, or even having read many books on architecture, before Castle Howard. He had become friendly with Sir Christopher Wren, who had similarly embarked on architecture as a comparatively understandable extension of his work as a mathematician. That would have been, of course, a considerable advantage. But we do not know of much else.

Castle Howard was vastly bigger than Goose-pie House, but the idiom was not dissimilar. It was rich and flamboyant, with an entrance hall rising into a great dome. But in the grounds of this immense baroque pile he would later build ramparts and fortifications that evoke the castle element of the name.

While building Blenheim Palace for the Duke of Marlborough, Vanbrugh developed an interest in the old Manor of Woodstock which lay in its grounds. This interest was not purely academic: he set about rehabilitating it as a residence for himself. Since this was done without authority from the Duke, he found himself in the position of having to explain his actions when Marlborough's implacably Vanbrugh-hating Duchess, Sarah, realised what he was at. Thinking on his feet, but also exploring a revolutionary aesthetic idea, he wrote a 'Memorandum' on the restoration of Woodstock Manor. In it, he sketched a philosophy that would come to colour the way in which many British people have regarded buildings ever since. Architecture, in the sense of mass, proportion and ornament, was not the only attribute by which they should be judged. Old structures should also be valued, he argued, for the associations that they aroused in the mind. This was the stirrings of the Picturesque tradition, that peculiarly English aesthetic, which has been expressed in the landscape gardening of the eighteenth century, the writings of John Ruskin in the nineteenth century and the conservation crusade in the twentieth century. Greenwich was to see the idea of the Picturesque, including a preference for asymmetry, applied to Vanbrugh's development on Maze Hill.

Vanbrugh's argument in favour of Woodstock Manor was based more upon the Manor's ability to move the mind than, in a conventional sense, to please the eye. He carried this notion over into his own architecture, when, for example, he remodelled Kimbolton Castle near Huntingdon. Kimbolton was an old house built round a courtyard, where the latest phase of work had been carried out by a provincial architect in the 1690s. But in 1707 the south front collapsed, and Vanbrugh rushed to the scene. 'As to the Outside,' he wrote to Kimbolton's owner Lord Manchester, 'I thought 'twas absolutely best, to give it Something of the Castle Air, tho' at the Same time to make it regular.' In Vanbrugh's œuvre, the 'Castle Air' is less familiar than the formal baroque manner, laden with columns and carved stone, of Castle Howard and Blenheim. Architecturally, the ingredients were simple. There were no columns, only rather plain volumes of masonry perhaps alleviated by rustication. Battlements break the skyline. Vanbrugh, of course, was no Victorian Gothic Revivalist: as his observation to Lord Manchester indicates, he did not seek to abandon the cardinal principle of symmetry. It was enough that battlements and a general impression of bulk should raise the appropriate associations in the mind. Nevertheless, the importance of the 'Castle Air' to him should not be minimised. He used it for his own house at Greenwich.

Vanbrugh had already rented a house at Greenwich for a year or two before building his new one, to be known as Vanbrugh's Castle. A friend referred to it as his 'country morsell', for Greenwich was still rural in 1717. But it was not isolated: a couple of Vanbrugh's friends already lived nearby. Various prosperous houses had been built in Greenwich in the previous century. As years went on, they reflected the change that overcame the area after the Civil War. No longer were the houses for the luminaries of the court, but for successful merchants, City men and sailors – with one or two owners, like Vanbrugh, who defy categorisation. In the 1630s, the Duke of Buckingham's secretary, Dr Robert Mason, had built a little red brick Dutch 'Hermitage', in the manner of the innovative Dutch House at Kew. 'The house is a wretched one,' judged John Evelyn, who had been invited over from Deptford.

However, that was twenty or so years after its construction, and he liked the view. Views, or prospects, were important in an age when, as here, special belvederes or other provision were made to take them. In the middle of the eighteenth century, Lord Chesterfield described the views from his bow windows in his house on Crooms Hill – on the other side of the Park from Maze Hill – as 'the finest prospects in the world'. The panorama from the top of Maze Hill must have been one of its attractions to Vanbrugh, since he gave his Castle a roof of lead flats that could be walked upon.

It is an intriguing irony that Vanbrugh's family should have originated from Ghent, given that the manor of Greenwich was for so many years owned by the Abbey of Ghent. Naturally, Vanbrugh already knew the area from his association with the Hospital, where he was now Surveyor (Wren had retired from the position in 1716). But it was not only work that persuaded him of the need for a country house. In January 1719, at the age of fifty-four, he got married.

It was an episode that allowed Vanbrugh's contemporaries some humour at his expense. Early in the courtship, when he was but forty-nine, Lady Mary Wortley Montagu reported from York (Vanbrugh had been staying at Castle Howard) to a friend: 'His Inclination to Ruins has given him a fancy for Mrs Yarborrough. He sighs and ogles that it would do your heart good to see him.' One would hardly know it from the disparaging reference to 'Ruins', but 'Mrs Yarborrough' was in fact unmarried (it was relatively common for women who were past girlhood to be styled as 'Mrs') and just the same age as Lady Mary Wortley Montagu herself – twenty-four. The old, or oldish, man who takes a much younger wife has been an object of other people's mirth since at least the days of Chaucer's *Merchant's Tale*. Vanbrugh was, furthermore, a wit. Some, then and since, have suggested he was a roué, though only from his having written mildly improper plays.

He therefore made a particularly satisfying object of ridicule. The Vanbrughs' domestic contentment seems to have been quite unaffected by it. There may have been thirty-five years between them, but everything suggests that their marriage was happy.

The new house was begun seven months before the knot was tied – perhaps even before he knew that he would marry. It still stands on Maze Hill, though the yellow London stock bricks have darkened to their usual grimy colour and it is now hemmed in by other buildings. When Vanbrugh acquired his lease of 'a Field and other Grounds' – a triangle of twelve acres carved from the Westcombe estate (once the property of the antiquarian William Lambarde) – it was still in the country, with just a few other houses round about. The Vanbrughs moved into their new home in 1720. The year before, Vanbrugh heard that, while he had been away, the Duke of Newcastle 'was pleas'd to Storm my Castle'. Nor could there be any doubting it was indeed a castle – original though the conceit must have seemed. From the Dover Road visitors to Vanbrugh Castle had first to penetrate a defensive ring of walls, bastions and gatehouse – a miniature version of the mock fortifications built at Castle Howard. Then, there was another gateway, just in front of the Castle, on the Greenwich side. The Castle itself comprised a four-square keep, with two square towers at the corners of the south façade (overlooking the field) and a circular one in the centre. The circular tower gave every floor a bow window, to take advantage of the view. There are battlements, a string course and a kind of scalloped corbel-table – all very medieval. The etiolated proportions do not suggest any great strength, but the relative height (it rises four storeys) gives a fairytale character – in the late twentieth century, reminiscent of Disney. Vanbrugh Castle might be called a revival for revival's sake. It is difficult to estimate its influence, but it must have struck

Vanbrugh Castle. As castles go, it was not large. But as Vanbrugh wrote, 'one may find a great deal of Pleasure, in building a Palace for another, when one shou'd find very little living in't ones Self'.

contemporaries as unprecedented. It can claim a place at the very beginning of the Gothic Revival that so delighted Horace Walpole and swept Victorian architects off their feet.

Despite its military bearing, this remarkable house is not large; nor are the rooms within it. As he wrote to 'old Jacob' Tonson, the publisher who had also been secretary of the Whiggish Kit-Cat Club, much frequented by Vanbrugh at one time: 'one may find a great deal of Pleasure, in building a Palace for another, when one shou'd find very little living in't ones Self.'

By 1722 Vanbrugh could report that he was 'now two Boys Strong in the Nursery'. He adored his children, in the way that older fathers do. Their own arrival necessitated expansion, with the building of new wings. Whereas the original castle had been fanciful in style, but symmetrical in form, symmetry was now thrown to the winds, in favour of Picturesque irregularity. It was not something that Vanbrugh ever tried in one of his larger commissions, but he could do it at home.

Nor was that all. Very soon after he acquired the lease of Maze Hill, Vanbrugh set about gathering other members of his family around him. Almost as soon as he began his own Castle, work started on another house on the site, probably for his youngest brother Philip, a captain in the navy and recently widowed. From earliest days, the house was called the Nunnery – which must have meant something to the Vanbrughs, though we can only guess at its significance now. In the next century it would have been called a bungalow: a spreading single-storey structure, with a little tower over the middle of it. Then came the *Castellulum Vanbrugiense* (little Vanbrugh Castle) for his 32-year-old brother Charles, already prosperous from a faintly shady career at sea and subsequent investments. It was called Mince-pie House – an echo of the Goose-pie House at Whitehall. There is not much that is obviously a mincepie about it. But it was a colourful conception, with a square centrepiece of five bays, a rusticated doorcase and circular side towers, again rusticated (on second thoughts the crenellated tops do suggest a piecrust). Like Vanbrugh Castle itself, these sibling mansions were built of London stock brick. Two further houses, the White Towers, were constructed out of patented white bricks supplied by a Fulham brickmaker to whom Vanbrugh had given financial backing. Altogether there were five houses on the estate. Each in a different idiom, they were dotted about the site in a thoroughly Picturesque manner.

They seem to have delighted Vanbrugh's older son Charles, which may have been part of the point (sadly, the younger of the two boys in the nursery, John, died at the age of a year). To Vanbrugh, one imagines that the sensations that passed through his breast as he went under the gateway included family warmth, amusement at his own architectural conceit, a sense of entering a self-contained world of his own making, relief after the externally imposed artifice of the town, and pride in his achievement.

He had half a dozen years to enjoy it, before his death of a quinsy in 1726. With his death the heart went out of the quirky assemblage of houses on Maze Hill – a family compound, as it would have been called later in the United States. Today only his own house survives.

As Much Honour
and Delight as This
World Can Give

MUCH OF THE GREENWICH which Vanbrugh knew
was a poverty-stricken slum. 'I took notice of several
good houses on the left hand [of the church] which
looked like habitations fit for Christians to live in,' writes the
author of a newspaper account of a journey through Greenwich to
Charlton Fair in 1700. 'But in some parts of the town the huts
were not bigger than wigwams, scarce big enough for a man to
lye at length in without putting his head or his heels in the chimney corner.' The food was just as bad. Greenwich was 'like a
Spanish Town', so short of fresh meat that, 'a Gentleman not long
ago, brought his Mistress down with a Design to lye all Night in
the Town, but was forc'd to go back to *London*, at seven a Clock
at Night, against Tide, because never a Publick House in the
Town could procure him a Supper.'

In 1710, after the collapse of the parish church of St Alfege's,
the people of Greenwich petitioned the Crown for help in rebuilding it. They claimed that the town had long been deserted by its
richer inhabitants, and the largest houses were empty. Nine-tenths
of the population were supposed to be seafarers. Tradesmen were
in trouble after having given long credit. Three thousand widows
and children had become a burden on the parish after the Great

Storm of 1703 had sunk many vessels; and yet more widows and orphans had been made when three of the ships led by Admiral Sir Cloudesley Shovell, returning from Gibraltar, struck rocks off the Scilly Isles. These figures must have been exaggerated; still, they suggest the poverty that had settled on the town, in contrast to the fine buildings erected in the royal park under the Stuarts. But at least the town got its new church.

Gradually the place acquired an overlay of gentility. Daniel Defoe wrote of the 'lustre of its inhabitants' when describing Greenwich in his *Tour through England and Wales*, published in 1724–6: 'there is a kind of collection of gentlemen, rather than citizens, and of persons of quality and fashion, different from most, if not all, the villages in this part of England.' There was a special Greenwich flavour to this gentility: a salty, leathery, gunpowdery note which came from the number of retired officers, from both army and navy, who resided there. As Defoe puts it:

Here several of the most active and useful gentlemen of the late armies, after having grown old in the service of their country, and cover'd with the honours of the field, are retired to enjoy the remainder of their time, and reflect with pleasure upon the dangers they have gone thro', and the faithful services they have perform'd both abroad and at home.

Several generals, and several of the inferior officers, I say, having thus chosen this calm retreat, live here in as much honour and delight as this world can give.

In addition to these retirees were the serving officers employed in the dockyards and arsenal. Altogether there was such a demand for good houses that 'the town of Greenwich begins to out-swell its bounds'. New streets were planned, the population grew, the new church, built only a dozen years ago, was already beginning to look small.

It was not only naval officers who had connections with the sea. Sir Ambrose Crowley had purchased what was to become Crowley House – the house built by Sir Andrew Cogan just before the Civil War and finished by the regicide Member of Parliament Gregory Clement – in 1704, and reconstructed it. 'Very great manufacturers of iron anchors, etc.,' was how Horace Walpole's antiquarian correspondent, N. Hillier, described the Crowley family in 1780. Thomas Pennant found the grounds of Crowley House littered with 'all kinds of iron manufactures'.

Greenwich was also becoming fashionable among people who had no connection with shipping and the sea. Lord Egremont, who lived at Charlton House, records the visits that he made to people in nearby Greenwich and Blackheath in his diary. In August 1731, he returned 'Mr Signoret's visit'. Mr Signoret was a merchant, and as such worked in the City; but he could spend 'much of his time at Greenwich, where he has a pretty house and garden, and a fine study of books. He married a daughter of the famous Dr Allix, French minister: a handsome woman and of great merit.' Later that month he 'returned the visits of Lord Pomphret, Sir Archibald Grant, and Mr Kellet, all on Blackheath'. The advent of Sir John Vanbrugh is evidence enough of the area's growing elegance; and as we have seen, some of his friends lived in the area already. The two white towers that he built on his fields were an early example of speculative building, having been constructed without a specific occupant in mind. They were not quite the first of this kind. For half a century there had been a demand for substantial houses, homes of the prosperous newcomers who were settling here; and where a demand exists, there will soon be speculators to take advantage of it.

Defoe had noted that in the 1720s Greenwich was extending itself 'to the top of the heath, by the way call'd Crum-Hill'. Building on Crooms Hill had begun nearly a century before:

externally, the oldest surviving house, now called Heath Gate House, appears to have been erected about 1630 by William Smith, hereditary Sergeant-at-Arms to the King. Smith comes down in Greenwich history as the founder of the Ship tavern. He was, therefore, a man of some enterprise, and Heath Gate House seems to have been a speculation. It was in the newly fashionable Dutch style, seen at Kew and elsewhere, well calculated to catch the eye of courtiers in need of lodging. Originally, Crooms Hill had been part of the gardens and orchards belonging to a house that lay near the river, built by the courtier family of Compton. Much of this land had been acquired by Sir Thomas Lake, who eventually succeeded Robert Cecil as Secretary of State. Lake was not an attractive figure: limited of talent, venal and unscrupulous. These qualities were not, in other people, a disadvantage at the Jacobean court, but in Lake's case they seem to have been, since his tenure of office was not only inglorious but brief.

But his grandson Lancelot, who was knighted at the Restoration of Charles II, deserves to be remembered locally as one of the earliest of Greenwich's developers. His activities were not confined to Crooms Hill; he seems to have built several houses round about, using his cousin Richard Ryder, who was the King's master carpenter, as architect. Sir Lancelot lived on Crooms Hill, in an old house called the Grange: it may once have been part of Paternoster Croft, a house that had belonged to the Abbey of Ghent. More recently it had been home to Edmund Chapman, Queen Elizabeth's chief joiner, and then the Lanier family of musicians. Lake remodelled this building, as well as erecting the house that is now numbers 16–18 on Crooms Hill. It may have been at the Grange that Sir William Boreman lived while he was replanting Greenwich Park. In 1662 the Grange was acquired by Sir William Hooker, a member of the Grocers' Company who would rise to be Lord Mayor of

London. Alderman Hooker had been one of a group of leading citizens in his parish who had consulted with Pepys about plague measures. Pepys had no great opinion of him: 'a plain ordinary silly man I think he is, but rich.' Furthermore, he found that he kept 'the poorest mean dirty table, in a dirty house, that ever I did see any sheriff of London'. That was in Eastcheap North, in the City of London. No wonder Hooker felt he needed a change of abode. In the garden of the Grange he employed Robert Hooke, the associate of Christopher Wren whose instruments caused poor Flamsteed such grief at the Observatory, to build a gazebo.

An engraving by Francis Place, made in about 1700, shows Crooms Hill from the Park. In this can be seen the house built originally by Robert Osboldston which Pepys, visiting Mark Cottle, had found 'very pretty'; it no longer exists. Cottle built 'five fair tenements' on the east side of the hill in 1702. A couple of years after Vanbrugh brought his wife to his Castle, a terrace went up at the foot of Crooms Hill, apparently a private venture to house captains of the Hospital. The architect John James built and lived in Park Hall, on Crooms Hill. It is to James that we owe the design of the steeple of St Alfege's Church. The original steeple had survived the collapse of the old church and had not been demolished: hence its exclusion from Hawksmoor's design. Alas, James's rather too dainty steeple does not possess the monumentality of the body of the church. Another resident was Sir James Thornhill, who worked for nineteen years on the Painted Hall at the Royal Hospital, and lived at 64 Crooms Hill from 1722 to 1724.

At the southern end of Crooms Hill lies what is now Chesterfield Walk, in the area of which Andrew Snape, the King's sergeant farrier, built three houses, in somewhat suspicious circumstances, given that the lease on the land had not actually been granted to him when work began. Snape belonged to a family whom Evelyn mentions as having been sergeant farriers to the sovereign for three hundred years. He published a book called *The Anatomy of an Horse* in 1683. But he was equally 'a man full of projects' and builder of the new tavern by the bowling green at Blackheath. If Snape hoped that the area would increase in fashionability because of the association with royalty, he must have been disappointed to discover that William and Mary, coming to the throne in 1688, had little interest in Greenwich for their own occupation. But this did not deter others from erecting four-square, quite stylish residences, such as Macartney House. Built in 1694, this was bought by the parents of General James Wolfe of Quebec, when he was twelve years old. Wolfe, educated in Greenwich, lived here when he was not soldiering, and it was from Greenwich that he left on his last expedition to Canada, in September 1759. After his death on the Plains of Abraham, his remains were brought home and buried in a vault below St Alfege's Church.

Next to Macartney House is the Ranger's House, built somewhat after its neighbour for Captain, later Admiral, Francis Hosier. Hosier was the son of a Deptford storekeeper, who had done well from victualling the royal ships (Pepys, as Secretary to the Navy, had contact with him). The young Francis went to sea at twelve or thirteen, and was a captain ten years later. At the brow of the hill, the house even now enjoys a fine view of the Thames: this prospect must have been ravishing before the banks of the river were developed. No doubt it was particularly pleasing to the eye of a sailor, though Hosier's choice of the site may also have been determined by a desire to get on in society; there were aristocrats like the 2nd Duke of Richmond living nearby. He furnished his house in walnut, with one or two mahogany pieces and what must have seemed the princely extravagance of a suite of silver furniture in the dining room. Seven or eight servants kept the

155

place going. Hosier was one of four thousand seamen to die of yellow fever while blockading Spanish treasure ships into the port of Porto Bello, in central America, in 1725 and is best remembered by Richard Glover's political ballad of some years later, 'Admiral Hosier's Ghost'.

There was a lengthy court case after Hosier's death, but the house was eventually bought by John Stanhope, younger brother of the Earl of Chesterfield. He was appointed a Commissioner of the Admiralty in 1748 – perhaps the naval connections of Greenwich had appealed to him. He appears to have spent large sums on improving the house. But in 1748 he died, leaving the house to Lord Chesterfield.

To begin with Chesterfield found the Blackheath property something of a burden. For one thing, while Greenwich was adequately fashionable, it was not nearly fashionable enough for Lord Chesterfield, who prided himself on knowing all the most glittering people in Europe. He would much rather his villa had been at Twickenham or Richmond, where Alexander Pope, the Countess of Suffolk and others added intellectual and social lustre. But within a few years he had fallen for the place. As deafness encroached, shutting him off from easy conversation with his contemporaries, it may have suited him to be geographically remote from society. And he had a fashionable house in Mayfair, built for him by the Palladian architect Isaac Ware. He referred to the Blackheath house on one occasion as his 'petite Chartreuse' (a monastery of the worldly Carthusian order) and on another as 'my hermitage'. He continued: 'This, I find, is my proper place; and I know it, which people seldom do. I converse with my equals, my vegetables, which I found in a flourishing condition.' As this letter suggests, he was seized by the *furor hortensis*, as he described it, 'and my acre of ground here affords me more pleasure than kingdoms do to kings'. Already on 23 December 1748 – the year that he acquired the house – he wrote to his friend Solomon Dayrolles, asking for 'seeds of the right Cantelupe melons. It is for Blackheath that I want it.' He was proud of the results, writing a few months later: 'I shall keep a little room for you at Blackheath, where I will refresh you with the best ananas and melons in England.'

By Chesterfield's standards, the house was not big. He made a joke of it to the Marquise de Monconseil, whose lodge in the Bois de Boulogne in Paris was called Bagatelle, or trifle. His own 'very small house' five miles from London 'I would have called Bagatelle had not I felt such a respect for yours; so I call it Babiole [meaning a bauble]'. In 1750 he went some way towards rectifying the defect of size by adding a large gallery on the south side, designed by Ware, running the full depth of the house, of one storey with no fewer than three bow windows – one for each of the external walls. 'Blackheath,' he wrote to Dayrolles, 'is now in great beauty. The shell of my gallery is finished,' and the three bow windows gave him 'three different, and the finest prospects in the world'. There were now eighteen servants to look after the house and its solitary owner. To the outside world, Chesterfield in his 'hermitage' presented a sage-like picture:

By wisdom purify'd, by age inspir'd,
For twice nine years in Greenwich groves retir'd,

as a verse in the *Gentleman's Magazine* expresses it. He himself did not feel that age was so very inspiring. 'Retirement was my choice seven years ago,' he wrote; 'it is now become my necessary refuge. Blackheath, and a quiet conscience, are the only objects of my cares. My little garden, the park, reading and writing, kill time there tolerably; and time is now my enemy.'

It was part of the Chesterfield code that he never intentionally committed the vulgar act of laughing. Nevertheless, a smile was permitted, and he was celebrated for his wit. When someone asked after Lord Tyrawley, who had taken the lease of Vanbrugh Castle from Sir John's widow, Chesterfield replied: 'Tyrawley and I have been dead these two years but we do not choose to have it known.' After Chesterfield's death, without legitimate issue, his house was inherited by his rackety godson, a distant cousin who became 5th Earl of Chesterfield. His period is remembered for a drunken dinner, with the future George IV present, when a ferocious dog called Towzer was released and savaged a footman, before being clubbed into submission by one of the party. In the mêlée Lord Chesterfield tumbled down the front steps, badly hurting his head. Early in the next century, Chesterfield House became the Ranger's House, the official residence of the Ranger of the Park.

In 1774 the insurance underwriter John Julius Angerstein built the country villa of Woodlands (now home to the local history library in Mycenae Road). Then thirty-nine years old, Angerstein's rise to a position of fortune had been meteoric. Born in St Petersburg, he had been apprenticed in a London counting-house at the age of fifteen before entering Lloyd's Coffee House. He quickly became the leading man in the industry, moving what was to become Lloyd's of London from the coffee house and becoming its first chairman. He was a man of method. He dressed always in the same uniform of blue coat, striped waistcoat, drab cloth breeches and buckled shoes. He talked little, often went to sleep during dinner, might well go to bed when a rout was taking place in his house, and insisted on his meals being served punctually, with no waiting for late arrivals. Angerstein's picture collection was purchased by the government after his death in 1823 and forms the basis of the National Gallery. He is buried in St Alfege's at Greenwich.

It is surprising that a man of such taste did not seek out a more distinguished architect than the one he employed: George Gibson. Gibson, the son of another architect of the same name, had local connections, and built himself a house on the other side of Blackheath, on Loampit Hill, in Lewisham. In this he deposited the collections of 'curiosities in Art' that he had gathered while travelling in Italy. The effect of the ensemble was indicated by the name of the 'Comical House' by which the dwelling came to be known. Gibson, according to an account quoted in Howard Colvin's *Biographical Dictionary of British Architects*, was too gentlemanly in his tastes to care much about building sites. 'He would rather sip his claret, drink his Madeira, chat about Art and Music, and take snuff with a gusto, than ascend ladders, tramp scaffolds to see how Briklayers filled in their work, or try the scantlings of wall plates and bond timbers … [like] the practical men of Sir Robert Taylor's working school.' It may have been a recommendation that George Gibson senior was employed by the future Queen Caroline, who was a friend of the Angersteins.

'The Princess is grown very coarse and … she dresses very ill, shewing too much of her naked person,' grumbled the antiquary Samuel Lysons, after one of Princess Caroline's frequent appearances at a Woodlands party. 'A Mrs. Weddel, who is large and unwieldy, came to the rout and was followed into the room by a little man of the name of Parrot. The Princess said "she should have brought him on her finger".' The humour of that sally was dissipated by her standing 'with her back to a table the whole time, which prevented every other person from sitting, this being the etiquette'. On another occasion she teased the artist Fuseli, who was staying at Woodlands, to such an extent that he left the next morning.

Friends such as the Angersteins must have viewed the Princess's arrival in the area – first at Charlton, then at Blackheath – with trepidation. The daughter of George III's sister, Augusta, and the Duke of Brunswick, she had a robust sense of humour, boisterous manners, slatternly habits and little regard for what anyone thought of her behaviour. Two of her brothers were weak in the head, and she herself was, by the conventions of Georgian England, more than a little odd. She was in an odd position. Before she married the Prince of Wales, he had contracted an invalid marriage to the Catholic Mrs Fitzherbert, and on her first arrival in Greenwich the Prince had made so little attempt to conceal his subsequent mistress, Lady Jersey, that he actually sent her to greet his bride. The Prince and Princess managed to produce a daughter, Princess Charlotte, but after that led separate lives, the Prince being free to consort with whom he chose, the Princess, not yet thirty, expected to deport herself as though still conventionally married to her errant husband. It was not in the Princess's nature to conform.

In the summer of 1798 she moved to Montague House, the lease of which her husband had taken from the Duchess of Buccleuch to provide a salubrious home for the little Princess Charlotte. The Duchess had written: 'I am afraid it is not in very good order, having been very long uninhabited. The situation, however, I flatter myself will make it agreeable to the Princess of Wales.' It lay next to Lord Chesterfield's old house, and had been built about the same time. In comparison to the palaces occupied by her building-mad husband, Princess Caroline's accommodation was rather modest, though it had the advantage of a second house at the end of the garden, built against the wall of the Park. This took its name of the Round Tower from a circular projection looking over the Park, whose rooms must have enjoyed panoramic views. It was useful as a lodging for a lady-in-waiting, her husband and a servant – or as a place of intrigue for Princess Caroline. The main house itself was distinguished by its greenhouse or conserva-

John Flamsteed, painted by Thomas Gibson in 1712. This portrait, does not suggest the ill health which dogged the first Astronomer Royal. The pugnacious lip hints at the chronic bad temper and argumentativeness which caused him to fall out with other scientists, including Isaac Newton.

A. C. Pugin's aquatint of Nelson's lying-in-state at Greenwich Hospital. The crowds of people wanting to pay their respects stretched all the way from Greenwich to London.

Opposite Princess Caroline of Brunswick, painted by Sir Thomas Lawrence in 1804. The Princess sculpted, hence the modelling tool in her hand. Some say Lawrence became her lover in the course of painting the portrait.

Canaletto's view of Greenwich, 1755. Nothing else captures the dignity of the project so well. Who would guess that the buildings took fifty-five years to finish, amid constant anxieties about money.

A hot-air balloon view from above One Tree Hill in 1845 clearly shows the sweep of the River Thames.

The Millennium Dome, the latest addition to Greenwich's great architectural tradition.

tory – a very Regency feature – reached directly from the Blue Room, the principal room in the house. Stables, kitchen gardens and outhouses were all located some five hundred yards from Montague House, next to a building called, from its Chinese roof, the Pagoda. This still stands in Pagoda Road, Blackheath.

To some, Montague House had, on first acquaintance, a rather melancholy appearance, partly because it was so well shaded by trees. The Princess did what she could to banish any such impression. It may seem that, with her romps, noisiness and 'pandemonium games', kissing games, Caroline was an unlikely friend for such a dry stick as John Julius Angerstein. With her 'very short neck, low stature, large and, as she dresses, not only prominent but ascending posterior', and her comical English ('Are you not glad to see me with my head upon my rump,' she once said, meaning 'on my shoulders'; *Rumpf* in German translates as 'body' or 'trunk'), she was an easy object of fun – and even friends, such as Lord Glenbervie whose words I have quoted, did not scruple to laugh at her. (Lord Glenbervie's wife was Caroline's mistress of the robes.) But for all of that, she had artistic tastes. She was skilled at such ladies' work as marbling paper, painting in watercolours and ornamenting tabletops by arranging dried flowers under glass. A portrait by Lawrence shows her wielding a modelling tool: very unusually for the age, she was an amateur sculptress.

Naturally she was much occupied by the decoration and, after three or four years, enlargement of the house. In this she could hardly compete with her husband's opulent, fantastic and ruinously expensive works at Carlton House, Brighton Pavilion and Buckingham Palace. But she did her best, employing, in the words of Miss Hayman, the long-suffering keeper of her privy purse who occupied the Round Tower, 'ten thousand workmen smelling of the humble humanity and stupid as posts and slow as snails'. She added a Gothic dining room, a new library and created a tented room, *à la turque.* The last would have appealed to her husband, if he had ever seen it. The inspiration came from the brilliant and heroic Sir Sidney Smith, whose picaresque naval career culminated in an action at St Jean d'Acre in which he captured all the French siege artillery at sea, mounted on the walls of Acre and, with a motley band of British and Levantine troops, repulsed Napoleon's siege. Sir Sidney, she wrote, 'furnished me with a pattern for [the room], in a drawing of the tent of Murat Bey, which he had brought over with him from Egypt. And he taught me how to draw Egyptian arabesques, which were necessary for the ornament of the ceiling.'

The Princess amused her friends by organising novel entertainments for them, such as an alfresco breakfast. Lord Minto found it 'extremely agreeable', despite 'a slight shower, which drove the white muslins for a few minutes into the house'. But the Princess's disregard for the norms of society went beyond open-air breakfasts. It was her practice, of an evening, to single out a man to share her conversation, and often the two of them would retire from the party, into a separate room or the garden. This invited comment; and the comment was not always without foundation. Her intimacy with Sir Sidney Smith went far beyond a discussion of tented ceilings. And he was but one of the many naval figures which Greenwich society could supply for her parties. Captain Thomas Manby was fitting out a frigate at Deptford in 1802: Sir Sidney was mortified to spot them playing footsie under the table one evening. In 1806 a public enquiry, or 'Delicate Investigation' into her life after her separation from the Prince of Wales was conducted, and the evidence, in so far as it reflected her general behaviour, was damning. We cannot be sure that the painter Lawrence became her lover when staying at Montague House – against convention – while painting two portraits. It hardly matters; there were so many others.

But Caroline was more than a rackety, over-boisterous vulgarian. There was a warmth and humanity to her, expressed in a love of children. This was much more than a Rousseau-esque affectation. At the Pagoda, she established a small nursery for orphans, winning the approval of the German educationalist Joachim Heinrich Campe when he visited in 1802. He described the garden and the Pagoda in his journal:

> I was transported with the elegance, taste and convenience displayed in the Pavilion, in which the dignified owner, who furnished the plan and the directions for every part of it, had solved the problem, how a building of but two floors, on a surface of about eighteen feet square, could be constructed and arranged in such a manner that a small family, capable of limiting its desires, might find in it a habitation equally beautiful, tasteful and commodious. The manner in which this has been effected deserves, in my opinion, the notice and admiration of professed architects.

The Princess directed the education of the children at the Pagoda and came to talk to them every day. They were 'clothed in the cleanest but at the same time in the simplest manner, just as the children of country people are in general dressed'. The children were evidently fond of her, and she did not strive to promote them into an impossibly exalted station in life: 'The boys are destined to become expert seamen; and the girls skilful, sensible, industrious housewives – nothing more.'

In the case of one act of charity, she went rather further. In the autumn of 1802, allowed only a weekly visit to her daughter Princess Charlotte, she asked her servants to keep an eye open for a baby that she could take into the house. As it happened, one was to present itself that very October, in the shape of a three-month-old boy called

Willie Austin. His father had recently been discharged from Deptford dockyard, as part of the economies that followed the Treaty of Amiens, bringing temporary peace with France. His mother hoped that the Princess could be persuaded to use her influence to reinstate him. She did not gain admittance to Princess Caroline, but her page offered Mr Austin employment in his wife's Pimlico laundry and, to ease the family's finances, the little boy was adopted. From this distance in history, it seems an act of compassion; to her contemporaries a 'strange whim', if not necessarily a malign one. But the last judgement depended upon the extent to which they regarded Caroline as a potential political nuisance. If she were to claim the baby as her own and legitimate, the boy could one day claim the throne. Hence the Delicate Investigation into the Princess's conduct at Blackheath.

George III, with whom she had been popular, made her Ranger of Blackheath, as a means of clearing some of her debts (it enabled her to let Chesterfield House). The findings of the Delicate Investigation killed the sympathy that he had felt for her. Caroline came to spend less and less time at Blackheath, forsaking her gallant sea-captains for the *bon ton* of the West End.

* * *

Among the more sober moments in the future Queen's career was the death of Admiral Lord Nelson, killed at the Battle of Trafalgar. On Christmas Eve 1805 his body was brought up the river to Greenwich. Greenwich was a doubly appropriate location for his lying in state. Not only was it about as closely associated with Britain's maritime history as it was possible to be, but Nelson had known it when he was alive. His body was laid in the Record Room of the Seamen's Hospital, while the walls of the Painted Hall were draped in black, and a dais, canopy and heavy curtains were erected. According to *Fairburn's Edition of the Funeral of Admiral Lord*

Nelson, a contemporary report of the obsequies, the setting for the 'melancholy spectacle' was achieved 'with peculiar taste and elegance; and was beyond all precedent, mournfully grand and impressive'.

The lying in state began after the New Year. The first mourners included the Princess of Wales, a usually boisterous figure who on this occasion, wrote Admiral Collingwood, 'remained several hours in contemplation and silent sorrow'. When she had gone, a 'few persons of respectability' were admitted. Then, for three days, the British public was given the opportunity to pay its last respects to its hero. The queues of people wanting to file past the coffin stretched all the way back into London. It is estimated that ninety thousand people paid their respects. The entrances to the Hospital were guarded by Volunteers and River Fencibles. Cheering greeted the forty-six seamen and fourteen marines who had fought under Nelson on the *Victory*, when they jumped ashore from their brig. In that emotionally expressive age, 'every eye' watching the scene was so moved by the combined feelings of 'rapture and agony' that it shed tears.

Eventually, the funeral procession that followed the coffin to its final resting-place in St Paul's Cathedral would include most of the great figures of the age. It was so long that the vanguard had already arrived at St Paul's before the last peers and others had properly left the starting-point in Whitehall.

But the departure of the coffin from Greenwich on 8 January 1806 had been even more dramatic. The night before had been squally, but the morning dawned bright and clear, and winter sunshine sparkled on the barges that were assembling to accompany Nelson's mortal remains. The leading barges were solemnly draped in black cloth, the one carrying Nelson in black velvet. Drums and trumpets sounded funeral music. All the state barges that could be mustered – the King's, the Lords Commissioners of the Admiralty's, the Lord Mayor's – manoeuvred into position.

Five hundred pensioners, all of whom had served with Nelson, preceded the coffin as it left the Painted Hall. At three o'clock, the body was carried down the stairs from the terrace of the Hospital. Just at that moment the skies darkened and a violent hailstorm exploded over the river like grapeshot.

The procession of barges stretched out for a mile, the oarsmen rowing bravely through the rain. At last it reached Whitehall steps. Four admirals gathered to hold up the canopy that would cover Nelson's coffin for the short journey to its overnight lodging in the Admiralty. And then the downpour stopped, the clouds parted and the sun burst forth. It seemed to be a piece of natural symbolism to complement the more florid attempts of the Lord Chamberlain's department, as though the gods of the watery element were angry at surrendering their hero.

The next day, which saw one of the most theatrically impressive ceremonies ever staged in Britain, belonged to London. But Greenwich, its history interwoven with the sea, kept the memory of it alive for longer. After the funeral, the famous funeral car, its prow imitating the *Victory* and its canopy supported by palm trees recalling the Battle of the Nile, was displayed in the vestibule to the Painted Hall. It stayed there until 1840, when it was found to have decayed so badly that it was broken up. By then a shrine of Nelson memorabilia had been established. The relics included the coat he had worn at the Battle of the Nile and the one he had worn at Trafalgar, complete with bullet hole, in 1845. Dr Beattie, the doctor who attended Nelson as he lay dying, became physician to Greenwich Hospital, wearing the bullet that had killed Nelson as a brooch.

It was a subject of national scandal when a thief, hiding behind one of the statues in the Painted Hall, wrenched the gold hilts off Nelson's dress swords (including the one that had lain on his coffin), forced the jewels from their scabbards and made off with such precious relics as Nelson's Order of the Bath and other decorations, along with his gold watch and seal. History repeated itself in 1950 when the gaudiest of all the decorations which Nelson was entitled to wear – and wear them he did – was stolen from the National Maritime Museum. This was the famous Chelengk, a diamond ornament given to Nelson by the Sultan of Turkey after the Battle of the Nile. But by far the sorriest tale uniting Nelson's memory with Greenwich concerns the shabby figure whom a Major Gordon met in 1811 as she shepherded half a dozen schoolchildren through Greenwich Park. It was Nelson's destitute mistress Emma Hamilton, with their daughter Horatia; it was Horatia's birthday, and she was being taken to meet some of the heroes of Trafalgar in the Hospital as a treat.

England was no kinder to the Princess of Wales. In 1814 she left the country. Montague House was demolished the next year. But she was remembered by her friends around Greenwich. When John Julius Angerstein's mother-in-law Mrs Lock visited Woodlands at the time of Queen Caroline's trial for adultery in 1820, her maidservants attended a concert of religious music held at the Green Man, the tavern that used to stand at the top of Blackheath Hill. Many ladies in the audience were seen to be wearing white bows in their hair as a symbol of the Queen's innocence.

* * *

While the royal soap opera at Montague House had been playing before the footlights of national publicity, Greenwich and Blackheath had both been making every effort to transform themselves from an impoverished fishing village (in Greenwich's case) and bare fields (in Blackheath's) into neat little suburbs. At the beginning of the eighteenth century, the Seamen's Hospital was edged by a surf of higgledy-piggledy timber-fronted houses, tumbling into mean streets and around odd little courts and inlets, bearing such richly prosaic names as Bugg's Pond, Fubb's Yacht (a beer house), Stocks Lane, Assiter's Yard, Barber's Court, Leach's Alley, Maiden Row and Graham's Passage. Romney Road, separating the Queen's House from Greenwich Park, had, alas, been built; but it ended in the Market Square, so that traffic heading for London from the east had to take a tortuous route through the town. As the Hospital itself came within sight of completion, the Commissioners turned their thoughts towards pushing back this tide of flotsam and jetsam which rose almost to their doors. To begin with, they did little more than erect handsome gates to the west of the site. This involved purchasing and clearing the intervening land to give Wren's architecture a little breathing space. Their main campaign of civic improvement came later. But this first blow was enough to make other concerns in Greenwich look to their laurels. Buildings such as the coaching inn the Spread Eagle smartened themselves up: it was rebuilt with stabling for sixty horses, a malt kiln and the stone archway to what used to be the coaching yard in 1780. The shops still identified themselves with pictorial signs – banned in the City of London since 1762 – such as 'The Yellow Boot, opposite the Church', to quote one letterhead. But developers were striking out into the pastureland that lay back from the river, imposing order and geometry on what had been fields. They emulated Bath, Buxton and the other great schemes of Georgian town-planning, but on a miniature scale.

In Greenwich the one attempt at grandeur is Gloucester Circus, designed by Michael Searles in 1790. Searles was a local man, the son of a surveyor, and it was as a surveyor that he first practised. He proved himself to be an architect of ability. The Circus, just off Crooms Hill, was intended to be exactly that: two crescents enclosing a central circle. But the development never took off sufficiently for the second of the crescents to be built. Even the single sweep of twenty-one houses that now exists took until 1809 to complete. There were plenty of crescents and circuses being built in Britain during these years, but these developments were pitched at the grandest end of society. The Greenwich Circus aspired to be nothing more than middle class. What is more, it broke away from the blandness of form that had characterised previous crescents and circuses (like most of its forebears, it was not a true circus, which would have been circular, but an oval). Elements recede and project in a somewhat syncopated rhythm (though the feeble little pediments at the ends are a weakness). So architecturally it had much to recommend it; but as a speculation, less so. Nevertheless, the experience gave Searles sufficient confidence to project a development in association with the landowner John Cator to the south of Blackheath: the semi-circle of fourteen houses which was named, with estate agent's bravado, the Paragon.

It was less than twenty years before that John Julius Angerstein had built Woodlands. Now the trend was not to create new little country estates, but to butcher the land that went with the big houses around Greenwich into manageable joints, to be cooked by developers and served up, with appropriate garnishes, in slices to the superior middle classes. The Paragon occupied part of the estate belonging to Wricklemarsh House, where Colonel Blount had nurtured his vineyard and developed his inventions. Later Wricklemarsh had been owned by Sir John Morden, the merchant who founded Morden College. About 1725 John James rebuilt it as a handsome box, its entrance shaded by a giant portico, for Sir Gregory Page, son of a dracoman (or interpreter) who had risen to become a director of the East India Company and a baronet.

In 1783, eight years after Sir Gregory's death, the estate was purchased by Cator. Brought up in Bromley, only a few miles away, he came from a prosperous family and was himself a shrewd businessman. He ran a profitable timber business from Mould Strand Wharf, on the site of what is now Bankside Power Station. A political opponent referred to him as 'a damned carpenter'. Clearly he was more than that. He became a Member of Parliament and knew, or was known by, various literary figures, the most prominent of them being Samuel Johnson. Johnson held Cator in esteem; he was the sort of no-nonsense individual who appealed to him. Johnson's friend Mrs Thrale found the carpenter in need of sanding and polishing. 'It is possible to gain great information from keeping him company; but his voice is so loud and his manners so rough that disgust gets the better of curiosity.' He had no use for the Hall, already having two other houses to live in, so he took the roof off and eventually demolished it. He may not have had any immediate thought of developing his land, but he was too good a businessman to pass up the occasion when it arose in 1793.

There had been, or would be, other Paragons. Searles himself had erected a terrace on what is now the New Kent Road bearing that appellation. Others can be found in Bristol and Richmond. But the Paragon at Blackheath is the one that most justifies the boast. It is a semi-circle of seven pairs of houses, each entered at the side, the ground-floor windows set into arches; each pair linked to the next by a single-storey Tuscan colonnade. Searles not only designed the scheme; he was the developer who took the risk. These houses sold more quickly than those in Gloucester Circus, and the development was complete by the time that Nelson's funeral cortège left the Royal Hospital in 1806. They were 'substantially built' dwellings, in the words of an advertisement for number 1 the Paragon which appeared in *The Times* in 1801 (the original occupant had lived there only a year):

170

The family apartments consist of two handsome drawing rooms, fitted up with great taste; a spacious eating parlour, a gentleman's room, library and boudoir; and excellent entrance hall and light staircase; eight family bedchambers, dressing rooms, water closets; and admirable nursery and store rooms complete. The servants' apartments are suitable and the domestic offices are of every description with good cellaring and dairy. The outdoor offices are laundry, men's room, stabling, coach house, attached farm yard, with every requisite for pleasure and economy.

These houses, for all their urbanity, still had a whiff of the country about them. Each came with nine acres, and the outside attractions extended beyond 'pleasant views in every direction, with lawn pleasure ground, cold bath, etc.' to include a productive operation that would supply the family with food. 'The kitchen garden is well stocked and in most excellent heart and the pasture land is immediately attached and in high condition for produce.' In an age when difficulties of transportation of food meant that it often arrived in poor condition, if not actually contaminated, growing vegetables and keeping cows were of more interest than just a hobby. Some of the houses had the benefit of fish ponds.

The Paragon is the nonpareil of Blackheath development, but it was not alone. It typifies the dismemberment of the country estates that proceeded with dignity in the Regency and early Victorian periods, and with rather less decorum thereafter. The Wricklemarsh estate became developed as the prestigious Blackheath Park in the first half of the nineteenth century. The character of the place was captured by the American novelist Nathaniel Hawthorne in *Our Old Home* (published in 1863 but recalling time spent in England in the 1850s). 'We were dwelling

The Paragon, Blackheath, in 1852. This crescent was begun in the 1790s. Each house had a nine-acre garden that could provide milk and vegetables.

in one of those oases that have grown up (in comparatively recent years, I believe) on the wide waste of Blackheath, which otherwise offers a vast extent of unoccupied ground in singular proximity to the metropolis.' The look of the streets, with their 'villas or boxes' occupied by businessmen, seemed more American than English.

> The scene is semi-rural. Ornamental trees overshadow the sidewalks, and grassy margins border the wheel-tracks. The houses, to be sure, have certain points of difference from those of an American design, though seldom of individual taste; and, as far as possible, they stand aloof from the street, and separated each from its neighbor by hedge or fence, in accordance with the careful exclusiveness of the English character, which impels the occupant, moreover, to cover the front of his dwelling with as much concealment of shrubbery as his limits will allow. Through the interstices, you catch glimpses of well-kept lawns, generally ornamented with flowers, and with what the English call rock-work, being heaps of ivy-grown stones and fossils, designed for romantic effect in a small way. Two or three of such village streets as are here described take a collective name, – as, for instance, Blackheath Park, – and constitute a kind of community of residents, with gateways, kept by a policeman, and a semi-privacy, stepping beyond which you find yourself on the breezy heath.

Given that Hawthorne was not, to say the least, an unthinking anglophile, it is a benign judgement.

Meanwhile the centre of Greenwich had been receiving attention. While the Commissioners of the Hospital had managed to erase the worst of the slums that lay around their building, the streets that lay immediately beyond the gates remained unwashed by the tide of taste. To the kindly eye of the painter, they might be considered picturesque. It was here that the poor of the town lived, and the lanes and courts had something of a Neapolitan air, the buildings crumbling, the alleyways festooned with washing, the inhabitants of the houses sitting on doorsteps. Charming in their way, but also malodorous, disease-ridden and squalid. The Commissioners bought them up, and drafted a Greenwich Improvement Bill to lay out roads and improve the approaches to the Hospital. It was passed as an Act in 1831, and Joseph Kay, the Surveyor to Greenwich Hospital, created Nelson Street, King William Street and Clarence Street (now College Approach). A new wing to the Hospital Infirmary, the Helpless Ward, was built over the ancient market-place, so a new market had to be erected. Assiter's Yard, Barber's Court and the others disappeared, along with Friars Road, Tavern Row, Taylor's Rents, Stagg Court and a host of other hovel-lined alleys. And in 1823-4 the neo-classical architect George Basevi built the new church of St Mary, to supply the need which Daniel Defoe had identified a century before, by the north gate of the Park. Henry H. Richardson, writing his guidebook to Greenwich of 1834, called it 'a neat edifice in the Grecian style of architecture … The interior is decorated in a style of elegance and chasteness superior to most new Churches.' It was demolished in 1935. Samuel Nixon's 1844 statue of William IV, 'the Sailor-King', now stands on the site.

ARCADIAN LIFE AMONG THE COCKNEYS

T HE OPEN SPACE of Blackheath was used for many things in the Georgian age. Various local militia regiments, such as the Blackheath Rangers, the Loyal Greenwich Volunteers, the Blackheath Volunteer Cavalry and the private army of five hundred men raised by Sir Gregory Page of Wricklemarsh House, exercised on the heath. In 1683 John Evelyn visited the first of the agricultural fairs that were held each year until the 1860s. He thought they were more London than country affairs, and he was right. In his book *The Heath*, the local historian Neil Rhind quotes an advertisement for a booth at an early fair. 'This is to give notice to all gentlemen, ladies and others, that there is to be seen from eight in the morning till nine at night, at the end of the great booth on Blackheath, a West of England woman 38 years of age, alive, with two heads, one above the other, having no hands, fingers, nor toes; yet she can dress or undress, knit, sew, read, sing. She has had the honour to be seen by Sir Hans Sloane, and several of the Royal Society. *N.B. Gentlemen and ladies may see her at their own houses if they please. This great wonder never was shown in England before this, the 13th day of May 1741.* Vivat Rex!'

Feats of athleticism aroused great interest. Various races were run in May 1717, including one between two wenches with the prize of a holland smock. An officer was so exasperated when a maltster on a horse blocked his view that he drew his sword; but the maltster broke his Toledo, bloodied his nose and generally proved the superiority of plain John Bull to arrogance in uniform. George Wilson's prowess as the 'Blackheath Pedestrian' attracted huge numbers of spectators, sideshows and even a small herd of elephants. He set out to walk a thousand miles in a thousand hours, and would have done it, if the authorities, known as the Black Beaks of Blackheath, had not arrested him, fearing a riot. The charge of walking for money on a Sunday did not stick, but he was not given the opportunity to complete his thousand miles. Another endurance sport on Blackheath was prize fighting.

Nothing, though, can compare to the golf played on Blackheath. Blackheath Golf Club is the oldest outside Scotland. In the eighteenth century, it was played principally by Scots, and it is possible that the association of the place and the game dates from the era of that Scot and golfer James I. The earliest written records of the Club date from 1784. It possesses a silver club dated 1766. Earlier golfers sometimes wore uniforms, such as the scarlet jackets and white waistcoats of the London Scots Society. Greenwich pensioners served as caddies. The wearing of red jackets became a club rule in the mid-nineteenth century when the other members of the public had to be made aware of the golfers' approach. Caddies walked in advance, carrying flags. The pressure on the heath required the Club to introduce local rules to meet sometimes difficult circumstances. Balls that fell on the cricket or football pitches had to be regarded as unplayable. 'Golfers must wait for people and conveyances to pass out of their way before playing.' There was even a rule covering balls that got stuck in a gas lamp.

While golfers strolled above, for seventy years the Blackheath Caverns played host to various activities, both dainty and debauched. They consisted of four chambers, hewn out of the chalk. From the moment they were discovered, wild theories were advanced as to their origin and history. One of the least fanciful is that they were dug by the Anglo-Saxon inhabitants of the area, wishing to hide from the Danes. But they were in fact created as recently as the fifteenth century, when chalk was quarried from the area. There had been other caves under Blackheath, causing alarm as subsidence swallowed up elm trees or horses.

Whatever the origin of the Caverns, they filled impressionable minds with the romance of remote ages. Sensibilities attuned to Edmund Burke's theory of the Sublime found them gratifyingly horrific. Candles were fitted up; balls and dances were arranged. The impresario who organised the 'Grand Bal Masqué' in 1850, a Mr J. Sleaman, boasted of the wonderful effect of the music at two hundred and eighty feet below ground. The penumbral lighting, combined with the generally thrilling air of the place, caused censure: anything might be happening in the shadows. Eventually, when somebody (or lack of oxygen) doused the lights completely during a masked dance and panic ensued, it was felt that enough was enough. The caverns were closed in the mid-1850s, a few years before the Greenwich Fair.

* * *

The Georgian architecture of Greenwich, with its decorous villas and neatly geometrical streets, might suggest that the earthiness associated with the Pepys era had been thoroughly tamed by politeness. This was certainly the image that P. Russell wanted to put across in *England Displayed*, 1769, when he described the town as 'one of the genteelest and pleasantest in England'. This opinion was repeated by Edward Hasted in his *History of Kent*, 1778, with the addition:

> The dryness and salubrity of the soil, the convenience of
> the park, the general pleasantness of the adjoining country,

and its near neighbourhood to the metropolis, contribute
to make it a most desirable residence for people of fashion.

There was an element of wishful thinking in this emphasis on the
polite qualities of the place. Blackheath retained an air of primitive
wildness, and the well-to-do must have felt relieved to cross it
without incident. There are many newspaper accounts of highwaymen. One of them, known as Jack of the Green, robbed three gentlemen's coaches in the summer of 1759. After he had galloped
away, one of the victims ordered his coachman to unhitch the
horses from the coach, and together they set off in pursuit. Jack of
the Green was not a master of concealment. They found him at a
drinking booth in Dartford. 'On searching him they found a brace
of pistols, loaded each with a brace of balls, a hat and a piece of
stocking sewed to it for a mask, a watch, eleven guineas, some silver, a pair of silver buckles, and two Spanish pieces.' He turned out
to be a sailor called Sam Walker belonging to the *Blenheim* man of
war. Even Greenwich Park was not perfectly safe. One Saturday in
June 1774, four footpads entered it by the north, south, east and
west gates and systematically robbed all the ladies taking their exercise there. Nathaniel Hawthorne rejoiced in Blackheath's lawless
reputation when he lived there in the mid-nineteenth century.
'Even now, for aught I know, the Western prairie may still compare
favourably with it as a safe region to go astray in.'

In 1774 the *Gentleman's Magazine* records a Greenwich riot
after some sailors, who had been pilfering from local gardens,
were locked up in the watch house. There was another riot in
1811, when four hundred Irishmen 'assembled and knocked
down every person in the streets they met with'. They stopped the
service in the church, and assaulted the congregation as it left.
These were some of the usual afflictions of port areas into which

arriving ships would suddenly discharge large numbers of sailors. Another concomitant was smuggling. One of the officers of the Queen's yacht lying off Greenwich seemed to have grown suddenly corpulent after a voyage in 1744; on being searched, he was found to have a quantity of lace concealed around his body. In the same year a man at Lee was charged with smuggling goods to the value of £15,000 – showing that it was a significant trade.

Greenwich Park, for all its avenues, Observatory and elegant adjacent streets, was not only the preserve of the prosperous families for whom Gloucester Circus, the Paragon and Blackheath Park were developed. It was somewhere that their servants and tradesmen, not to mention seamen, dockyard workers and artisans, could take their relaxation too. There was much clicking of tongues on the part of the genteel element at the lack of propriety evident in some of the demotic pastimes, such as tumbling down the Giant's Steps. To do this, men and women joined hands and ran down the bank from the top of Castle Hill. Inevitably they fell over and ended up in a highly immodest tangle of arms and legs. Women's dress was disarrayed, and undergarments – if worn – were put on view. Contemporary prints suggest that some lubricious individuals haunted the spot, simply to observe this display of feminine indecorum. Tumbling may have been vulgar, but it was invigorating. A piece of doggerel attached to a print entitled *Greenwich Hill or Holiday Gambols* urges the polite society of the West End to give it a try:

> Ye sweet scented Sirs who are sick of the Sport
> And the stale languid follies of Ballroom or Court,
> For a Change leave the Mall and to Greenwich resort:
> There heightened with Raptures which never can pall
> You'l own, the Delights of Assembly and Ball
> Are as dull as Yourselves, and just nothing at all.

Holiday Gambols on Greenwich Hill,1761. On the left a fiddler plays to a sailor (wearing 'slops', in the form of a divided skirt) with his lass. Men and women tumble down the hill behind, their clothes awry.

But tumbling was a risk sport. There were accidents, as on a Tuesday on 4 April 1730, when, according to the *Daily Journal*, crowds of Londoners 'diverted themselves' by running down the hill beneath the Observatory: 'one of them, a young woman, broke her Neck, another ran against one of the Trees with such Violence that she broke her Jaw-bone and a third broke her leg.'

Twice a year, probably from the beginning of the eighteenth century, the boisterousness of tumbling swelled into the organised mayhem of Greenwich Fair. This was one of the events of the London year. Even the French philosopher Voltaire visited it, entranced by what he took to be 'people of fashion' – who turned out to be only the servant girls, apprentices and other townspeople of Greenwich dressed in their best for the fair.

That was in 1726. Then there was a racetrack, for the use of both equines and humans, but the scale of the fair was still manageable and the atmosphere generally sedate. Respectable people went to meet each other, dine in specially erected booths, listen to music and dance quadrilles. But in the second half of the century the crowds coming to the fair were so great that they could not easily get through the entrances into the Park. The tone degenerated. What might be described as the tumbling classes got the better of the solid citizens, who stayed away, locking their windows and doors. An account in *The Gazetteer* describes how, in May 1776, the road from London was lined with every sort of conveyance, containing pickpockets and disreputable women. Once the Greenwich Railway had opened in the next century, as many as two hundred thousand people poured into the fair.

Posing as distinctly older than his twenty-three years, Charles Dickens, describing the fair in the *Evening Chronicle* in 1835, evoked the rackety conveyances into which Londoners – himself included – crowded to visit the Fair, and return from it, supposedly in his 'earlier days'.

We cannot conscientiously deny the charge of having once
made the passage in a spring van accompanied by thirteen
gentlemen, fourteen ladies, an unlimited number of
children, and a barrel of beer; and we have a vague
recollection of having, in later days, found ourself the
eighth outside, on the top of a hackney coach, at
something past four o'clock in the morning, with a rather
confused idea of our own name, or place of residence. We
have grown older since then, and quiet, and steady ...

In the thick of the fair, the weight of humanity compressed fair-
goers into a single, unified mass, assaulted on all sides by, and
contributing to, a cacophony of sound.

Imagine yourself in an extremely dense crowd, which
swings you to and fro, and in and out, and every way but
the right one; add to this the screams of women, the shouts
of boys, the clanging of gongs, the firing of pistols, the
ringing of bells, the bellowings of speaking trumpets, the
squeaking of penny dittoes, the noise of a dozen bands,
with three drums in each, all playing different tunes at the
same time, the hallooing of showmen, and an occasional
roar from the wild beast shows; and you are in the very
centre and heart of the fair.

Adding to the hubbub would be the boom of preachers decrying
the licentiousness of the event. There were plenty of others who
shared their view.

The chief amusement, mentioned time and again, was scratching.
The trick was to buy a little serrated wheel, made of wood, at the
end of a wooden stick. You then came up behind someone and ran it
over his or her back. The noise was supposed to make the victim

believe that his clothes had been torn. Scratchers were such a feature of the fair that one can hardly imagine that there were many people innocent enough to be caught out. Still, it was all part of the general hilarity. A more sedate pleasure was to look through the telescopes set up by Greenwich pensioners on the top of Castle Hill, offering views of the other bank of the river for a halfpenny. The principal feature of interest, in the previous century, was the gibbet on the Isle of Dogs, where the bodies of pirates swung in their chains. Naturally, great quantities of rum, brandy and gin were consumed and the public houses were thronged, fuelling the sort of misbehaviour that culminated in a riot of drunken soldiery in 1850; it was subdued by a combined force of policemen and mounted militia.

It was at Greenwich that the first 'Voyage Volante', or rising and descending roundabout, was brought before the public, in 1835. Two men underneath the machine turned a central mast, from which four boats hung on beams. The famous Wombwell's menagerie was there, with its elephants, freak shows, 'Intelligent Pig' and Wallace, the first lion to be born in captivity in Britain (born in Edinburgh, it was named after William Wallace, the Scottish patriot). 'No one probably has done so much to forward practically the study of natural history amongst the masses,' pronounced *The Times* in the obituary that followed Wombwell's death in 1850. John Ruskin, having suffered a childhood drained of almost any stimulating experience, confessed in *Fors Clavigera*: 'One of the nearest approaches to insubordination which I was ever tempted into as a child was a passionate effort to get leave to play with the lion cubs in Wombwell's menagerie.' At Greenwich, Wombwell was not allowed undisputed mastery of the animal shows; his great rival Hilton would also bring his menagerie, its lion tamer being a black man and former sailor called Macomo. Likewise Saunders came with his Royal Circus, performing equestrian stunts.

'The dwarfs are also objects of great curiosity,' wrote Dickens, 'and as a dwarf, a giantess, a living skeleton, a wild Indian, "a young lady of singular beauty, with perfectly white hair and pink eyes", and two or three other natural curiosities, are usually exhibited together for the small charge of a penny, they attract very numerous audiences.' Perhaps an even greater attraction was Richardson's Theatre. At one time it may have been set up in the Park, but its more familiar location was an immense booth beside Creek Bridge, a confection of canvas, red serge draperies and brass ornaments, all lit by thousands of glittering candle-flames behind different coloured shades. There might be an overture, melodrama, three murders and a ghost, a pantomime and a comic song – not bad for twenty-five minutes.

It was all rather too uproarious for the more established citizens of Greenwich. They began their campaign to close the fair in 1825, but the showmen, stallholders and crowds kept coming. Eventually, the forces of Victorian propriety proved too much for the fair, and it was shut down in 1857. By then, Richardson, Wombwell and most of the other principals of the big shows were dead. Their entertainments were passing out of favour, as travelling theatres gave way to permanent ones and the public was less easily taken in by talking pigs and lion-headed ladies. 'The spirit of public enquiry which marks the age has been fatal with regard to the wonders of Greenwich Fair,' opined the *Illustrated London News* in 1850. Though the crowds do not seem to have diminished much in the last years, there was now less need for a great popular jamboree to take place so close to London, since the railways had made it possible for holiday crowds to reach seaside towns such as Margate and Brighton.

Nathaniel Hawthorne, living in Blackheath Park, witnessed the very last of the Greenwich Fairs, finding it distasteful and malodorous. The seething, whistle-tooting, brandy-quaffing, shouting, familiar press of people, which Dickens enjoyed with gusto, was barely endurable to Hawthorne's fastidious temperament.

Yet his general asperity in his comments about English life make his appreciation of the daily scene in Greenwich Park, with its crowds of forthright, open, gutsy Londoners, an even greater accolade than they would be from another writer.

> They adhere closer to the original simplicity in which mankind was created than we ourselves do; they love, quarrel, laugh, cry, and turn their actual selves inside out with greater freedom than any class of Americans would consider decorous. It was often so with these holiday folks in Greenwich Park; and, ridiculous as it may sound, I fancy myself to have caught very satisfactory glimpses of Arcadian life among the Cockneys there, hardly beyond the scope of Bow-Bells, picnicking in the grass, uncouthly gambolling on the broad slopes, or straying in motley groups or by single pairs of love-making youths and maidens, along the sun-streaked avenues.

It is a novel definition of Arcadia, but Arcadia all the same.

All Honour
to the Enderbys

FOR FOUR HUNDRED YEARS, the kings and queens who had stayed here, built palaces, laid out gardens, received dignitaries, alighted on the steps by the river, or extended their patronage towards the Observatory and the Naval Hospital, made Greenwich shine beneath the lustre of their presence. With the departure of Princess Caroline, Greenwich lost its connection with royalty. But that only freed it to participate more fully in the dynamic developments and ideas that gave shape to the nineteenth century. Almost every one of them finds at least an echo, sometimes a shout, at Greenwich. Engineering, through the industries that came into being on what was once thought of as the manor of Old Court, but would become a river-edged promontory hectic with industrial activity, before its present incarnation as the site of the Millennium Dome; empire, because of Greenwich's continuing association with the sea and everything to do with it; railways, as a result of the very first railway line in the metropolis – indeed, the first suburban line in the world – being built between London Bridge and Greenwich. For eleven years the Borough's Member of Parliament was no less a figure than William Gladstone, the Prime Minister. Thanks to the Royal Observatory, Greenwich was indelibly associated with the standardisation of time, which separates the fast-moving, industrialised, modern world from the haphazard, agriculturally based one that preceded it. And through it all, in this heroically energetic age, moved the river, always the river, as fundamental to the identity of Greenwich as it had been at the time of the Romans.

* * *

If you bought tea in nineteenth-century London, it might have come wrapped in a puzzle paper. The puzzle was a sort of pictorial riddle, enchanting to look at if not always easy to solve. One of them, a great favourite, shows Napoleon III being carried to France on the back of an enormous crow. This was an allusion to Captain M. Crow, whose fishing smack transported the future Emperor back to his homeland, once the Revolution of 1848 made it safe for him to return. Captain Crow was one of the fishermen who worked out of Greenwich. 'On retiring from the sea he opened a fish shop in Turpin Lane, and sold very fine fish,' reminisced Mrs Thomas Norledge in 1915. 'I remember him well.'

Appropriately Greenwich's great emblem from the days of sail – the *Cutty Sark* – preserves Captain Crow's association with tea. It was built as a tea clipper, in an age when enormous prestige was attached to the ship that could perform the journey to China in the least time. The ship's name is derived from Robert Burns's poem 'Tam O'Shanter', in which Tam is pursued by witches as he rides drunkenly home. The fastest witch, young and beautiful, wore only a short linen shift, or 'cutty sark', and grasped the tail of Tam's mare before he managed to escape. Sailors loved the legend, and would make a grey mare's tail from an old end of rope and put it in the outstretched hand of the ship's figurehead. As her first master declared: 'She was the fastest ship of her day, a grand ship, and a ship that will last forever.' But when the *Cutty Sark* was launched in 1869, steam had already begun to replace sail. She carried her last cargo of tea in 1877. Then she discovered a new career in the wool trade to Australia, and in the late 1880s and early 1890s made the fastest passage home several times.

Captain Crow and the other Greenwich fishermen were the inheritors of a tradition which stretched back for centuries to Greenwich's first settlers. The Greenwich parishioners who petitioned Parliament in 1710 for a new church, after the collapse of the old St Alfege's, could claim that nine-tenths of the population were seamen – an exaggeration in which there lay a kernel of truth. Their successors sailed in the navy, in merchant ships and on the lighters that distributed the huge quantities of goods arriving in the Port of London from around the world. The fishing fleet clung at first to the Thames, its estuary and the coastal waters around its mouth; but when the method of fishing the seabed with a trawl was developed in the early nineteenth century, they roamed as far as Iceland and the Faroes in their fishing smacks. A rich hunting ground was the Dogger Bank, east of Yorkshire. The Greenwich fishermen were so well known in the ports that lay nearest to it that they were asked to help develop one of them. A new dock had been built at Grimsby; before it opened in 1845, the directors of the company which owned it met a party of Greenwich captains, in the hope of persuading them to make it their local base. They even made one of the first fishing smacks to be powered by steam, the *John Ellis*, available to them as an inducement.

They accepted the invitation, as well as the *John Ellis*. (The new-fangled *John Ellis* was not a success as a steamer; thinking that the noise of the engines disturbed the fish, the Greenwich sailors had it converted to old-fashioned sail.) For years the Greenwich men jealously guarded their right to precede all other boats out of the harbour. 'When the dock gates opened, Captain McBride, the first dockmaster, could be heard shouting, "Greenwich men first",' remembered Mrs Norledge, whose husband was an official of the company. 'I have seen the dock crowded with smacks, ready for sea, which would draw in close to make a waterway for a few Greenwich smacks to pass first. Compliments were very plentiful, which the Greenwich men would receive with a bow; and the old captain – eye steady, hand on tiller, hat raised and a smile of triumph on his lips – would make for the open sea.' The Greenwich men would ply between home and Grimsby, until home actually became Grimsby and they forgot Greenwich altogether.

Before the defection of the fleet, the fish landed at Greenwich included shoals of tiny sprat-like whitebait. They were much prized by the Victorians, and fuelled an appetite for whitebait suppers, served, most famously, at the Ship Hotel and Trafalgar Tavern on the waterfront. These whitebait feasts became a great London tradition. The whole Cabinet, Liberal or Tory, would assemble in an upper room of one of these pubs (the Trafalgar for Liberals, the Ship for Conservatives) to enjoy them. They were also popular with writers and artists. Dickens was fêted at the Trafalgar Tavern after his return from his first American visit in 1842. 'There is no next morning hangover like that which follows a Greenwich dinner,' he moaned. And it was to Greenwich that Bella, heroine of his *Our Mutual Friend*, insisted that her Pa should take her out to dinner, after she had bought him a new outfit and provided him with money for the outing.

The little expedition down the river was delightful, and the little room overlooking the river into which they were shown for dinner was delightful. Everything was delightful. The park was delightful, the punch was delightful, the dishes of fish were delightful, the wine was delightful ... And then, as they sat looking at the ships and steamboats making their way to the sea with the tide that was running down, the lovely woman imagined all sorts of voyages for herself and Pa.

To judge from contemporary illustrations – and it says something for the fame of these dinners that they were recorded pictorially – the atmosphere of these whitebait dinners was relaxed, convivial of course, the mood owing something to the almost seaside nature of the fishing port. The whitebait had to be served fresh. So fresh, in fact, that they were kept alive in water, fished out with a skimmer, then rolled around in a large napkin containing flour, and tossed into a cauldron of bubbling lard. Just two minutes' cooking, never more. 'The rapidity of the cooking process is of the utmost importance and if it be not attended to, the fish will lose their crispness,' opined John Timbs in *Club Life of London*, with reference to the Trafalgar's whitebait dinners. 'At table, lemon juice is squeezed over them and they are seasoned with cayenne pepper; brown bread and butter is substituted for plain bread and they are eaten with iced champagne or punch.' Who could resist them?

The architecture of the Trafalgar, designed by Joseph Kay in the year of Queen Victoria's accession, 1837, echoed this mood of relaxation, with its canopies and loggia, and general air of taking a liberty with the classical conventions. Men sprawled across chairs, threw their arms around each other in camaraderie, drank too much. Women do not seem to have featured very much. The Ship staggered on as an inn until 1941, when it sustained a direct hit by a German bomb; the site is now occupied by the dock containing the *Cutty Sark*. The Trafalgar still operates, its popularity drawing a veil over a period after 1890 when it ceased to function as an inn, becoming variously the Royal Alfred Aged Merchant Seamen's Institution, a working men's club and a block of flats. When it closed (temporarily) in 1890, a valediction was published in the *Kentish Mercury*. 'There are few of us of middle age who do not know something of the enjoyment of the exquisite dinners that were served in its public and private rooms of a balmy summer evening as the breezes from the

The Greenwich Dinner. A Convivial Moment.
This *Punch* cartoon depicts gentlemen
'under the influence of whitebait'.

Thames on the spring tide brought the refreshing flavour of sea salt,' wrote the *Mercury*. Was every evening balmy? Was a tang of salt really detectable above the other odours of the Victorian river? The jaunty architecture of the Trafalgar seems to tell us yes.

In size, whitebait are among the smaller fry to be harvested from the sea. Greenwich men went after not only them, but the very largest creatures of the deep – whales. And sometimes, the whales came to Greenwich. This was the case in 1273 when a whale, described as twelve 'toises' in length and five in girth (a toise being a length of very nearly two metres), was captured at Greenwich, and taken to London Bridge to be cut up. Another whale appeared at Greenwich in late 1658. Not only was it so extraordinary an arrival that people thought it must be an omen presaging Oliver Cromwell's death, but a pamphlet was published recording the event in graphic terms. The title alone unburdens a quantity of fact: *London's Wonder. Being a most true and positive relation of the taking and killing of a great Whale neer to Greenwich the said Whale being fifty eight foot in length, twelve foot high, fourteen foot broad, and two foot between the Eyes ...* The whale was first spotted by a boy, who was frightened to see 'such a Monstrous fish'. The boy told some watermen, who immediately armed themselves with harpoons, hatchets, billhooks and anything else they could lay their hands on. Then, 'stripping off their Doublets and Breeches, [they] went only in their Shirts and Drawers to be light and nimble at their worke'. The harpoons stuck into her, but came out again; the watermen stabbed her with spears, someone fired a couple of bullets into her, various anchors were flung at her, and eventually a fisherman lodged a little anchor in her nostril, which stuck fast. 'Whilst she was in this extasie and danger of death she would sometimes bounce above the water as high as a house, and down she would sinck into the Thames again, then up again leaping and tossing her body above the water, sometimes eight or nine foot high.' When, after further gory stratagems, she was killed, she became an instant marvel, with all London wanting portions of her flesh as souvenirs.

> Some bought peeces as big as a man's middle, and some took lesser peeces to shew to their neighbours, friends and acquaintance, that what is reported concerning this hugeous whaile, is an absolute truth; and as a monument of Remembrance, they do both safely and securely lock it up, esteeming more rarely of it, than a dish of Anchovis, Salmon, or Lobsters, that is a present for a Lady, for although a Whale be not good to eate, it is novelty, and very strange and much more stranger to be cacht in the River of Thames so neere to London bridge.

For all the commerce on the nineteenth-century river, and the pollution inside it, the spout of confused whales was a spectacle that once or twice astounded Greenwich residents in the Victorian era. Perhaps it reflects the skills that local people had in whaling that, when one appeared off Deptford in 1842, it was quickly despatched by five watermen. Measuring fourteen feet six inches, it was thought to have gone 'blind in the river while in pursuit of herrings' – though whales only eat plankton. A much larger whale, all of sixty-six feet seven inches, was chased aground at Woolwich in November 1899. At first a wonder, the huge animal soon presented problems of disposal, which became increasingly acute as decomposition set in. (When the body of the whale burst, it revealed two calves, still just alive.) Curiously, another whale beached itself at Woolwich a few days later. According to a report in *The People*: 'About two o'clock the crew of the steam tug Empress fastened a rope to it, dragged it off the beach, and took it in tow with the intention of consulting the Thames Conservancy as to what was to be done with the monster.'

Catching a whale off
Deptford pier in 1842.

Whaling vessels had been sailing from the Thames since the eighteenth century. Some time in the first years of the nineteenth century the whaling firm of Samuel Enderby and Sons established a rope and sail manufactory on the west of the peninsula of East Greenwich, the tongue of land looped by the Thames at the top of which the Millennium Dome has arisen. Enderbys had been trading in whale oil for years. Originally they had simply bought it from the Nantucket men, and it was the latter who incurred all the terrible risks of the hunt. This trade was disrupted by the American Revolution: the vessels from which East India Company tea was thrown into Boston Harbour in 1773 belonged to Enderby – the tea was to have been their return cargo. This may have spurred the company to investigate alternative sources of supply. They began to test the southern hemisphere for whales. They found them, and a flotilla of Enderby ships set off to reap the reward. This time the outward cargo was made up of convicts, destined for Australia. These ships sailed far into the Antarctic. Their presence is commemorated in the name of Enderby Land given to a black outcrop of mountain rising out of the icefloes. One Enderby ship, the *Britannia*, had Thomas Melville of Boston as its captain. His grandson, Herman, would be the author of *Moby Dick*. 'All honour to the Enderbys,' wrote Melville in that great work. The narrator of the book, Ishmael, believed that the house of Enderby, 'in my poor whaleman's opinion, comes not far behind the united royal houses of the Tudors and Bourbons, in point of real historical interest'.

On the other side of Greenwich, at Deptford, the dockyard continued as a building yard, long after the draught of the warships made it impossible for them to be fitted out there. Naval stores such as timber, pitch, tar and hemp could be bought at good prices there, since the ships bringing them from overseas could be sure of collecting another cargo from the London docks.

River-built ships enjoyed a premium in the eyes of sailors. There were boat-building yards on the peninsula: the National Company for Boat Building by Machinery declared its purpose in its title, though it seems not to have prospered, being taken over by the more famous firm of Maudslay, Son and Field, from Lambeth, in 1865. Maudslay's continued building quite sizeable ships at Greenwich until 1872, before the yard was converted into a boiler-making works. In between boilers they managed also to build the Great Wheel for Earl's Court in the 1890s. The works closed in 1900. Then there was John Penn and Company, makers of marine engines, who were later absorbed by the Thames Ironworks and Shipbuilding Company. In 1911 the latter were responsible for constructing the last battleship to be built on the London river, the *Thunderer*; the yard where this took place lay at Bow Creek opposite Greenwich, on the north bank of the river. It was near the spot where Isambard Kingdom Brunel's immense leviathan, or rather white elephant, the *Great Eastern,* was constructed, no doubt with Greenwich men supplying labour. It must have made an extraordinary sight, dwarfing all other boats on the river, marooned after completion for several months while the great engineer worked out the means of launching it.

There was also boat-building on the marsh where the Millennium Dome now stands. Hundreds of years ago, the peninsula, formed by a loop in the Thames, had been too boggy for any practical use. At one time, before the course of the Thames took on a regular outline, it was probably as much part of the river as of the land; it would have been regularly flooded if not permanently under water. Its Tudor landowners dug a system of dykes, ditches and sluices which succeeded in draining part of it. It could now be used to graze animals, and Henry VIII rode out from Placentia to hawk there. In the Elizabethan age, a large portion of the peninsula was

John Penn and Sons, Engine Works, on Blackheath Road, in 1863. They supplied marine engines to shipbuilders worldwide. John Penn Jr is first right in the foreground.

owned by the antiquary William Lambarde, otherwise remembered as the builder of Queen Elizabeth's College. He used to be commemorated here through the embankment he erected to prevent flooding, originally called Lambarde Wall and then corrupted to Lombard Wall. Occasionally the river claimed back its own. Some time before 1600 – perhaps in Lambarde's time – it took a large bite out of the flank of the peninsula by flooding some of the land. The unwelcome inlet was known on old maps as the Great Breach or (from its shape) Horse Shoe Breach. In the early seventeenth century the Court of Sewers for East Greenwich was established to regulate the draining of the marsh. A map of 1745 shows the only buildings on the peninsula to be a watch house and what was called the 'New Magazine'. The latter was a powder magazine, which stood near the site of the future Enderby's Wharf.

Not far away was Execution Dock, moved from Wapping in the eighteenth century. It consisted of a metal cage surrounding a gibbet, where river pirates, hanged, would be left in their chains while three tides passed over them. There were three cottages beside Enderby's Wharf, and some others, as well as the Pilot public house, near Ceylon Wharf, an old landing stage whose name reflected the exotic destinations familiar to Greenwich seamen. The Pilot had been built in 1801. The marsh had been chosen as the site of the powder magazine because almost nobody lived there. (The handful of people who did so understandably objected to the magazine's dangerous state in a petition of 1759.) The marsh has remained sparsely populated ever since. But follow the path that runs along the Thames, connecting the Millennium Dome to the centre of historic Greenwich, and you will see that this promontory, so close to London, attracted its share of industry. An ever-shifting band of enterprises – brave ventures, profitable ventures, disastrous ventures, outposts of concerns based elsewhere, flourishing, closing, being bought by other companies, their fortunes so accurately reflecting the market provided by the Victorian world – sprang into varying degrees of life, for varying lengths of time. Many of them were connected with shipping. Others were supplied by the river. Some still prosper: next to the Millennium Dome site a gravel works still piles up hillocks of stones. Most are ghosts.

One of the most attractive products to be built on the peninsula were the sailing barges that, with their ochre-coloured sails, made such a picturesque sight on the Victorian river. To the men who owned them, the appeal of the barges was that they could go almost anywhere, because their draught was so shallow, and with their flat bottoms they could sit upright on a beach or on mud when the tide was out. There could be as many as eight thousand barges working the Thames at any one time. They carried every kind of cargo, including hay from the Essex countryside into London to feed the enormous numbers of horses in the metropolis, and horse manure back to Essex for the fields. Hay would be built up into towering stacks, upon which stood a mate or boy to tell the skipper – whose view was filled with nothing but hay – how to steer. The firms that built the sailing barges also made the 'dumb barges', or lighters – barges without any independent means of propulsion – which can still be seen snaking their way along the river, in procession, behind tugs.

There was a tarry smell – sometimes literally – about a number of businesses on the peninsula, beyond those that actually built boats. As well as their wharfs, the Enderbys owned a factory to make rope. When iron cable began to replace hemp, the Camberwell firm of William Kuper and Company opened a works at East Greenwich to produce it. Most of their production was used as rope would have been; but the factory also had the distinction of producing much of the vast length of electric cable, for telegraph, that was laid beneath the Atlantic to link Britain and the United States. Laying this cable was one of the great triumphs of Victorian engineering, and it took four attempts to get it right. For the first two, half of the cable was embarked on each of two ships; in the summer of 1858, on the second try, a telegraph message was sent across the Atlantic. But the euphoria that this caused was short-lived, since within a month the cable had broken and could not be repaired. Nothing daunted, the promoters raised more money and ordered a heavier cable. There were disadvantages in using two ships, so they commissioned the only ship in the world big enough to carry the 22,500 tons of cable: the *Great Eastern*. The ship could not sail until 1865, due to the American Civil War. When it did so, the cable broke and it had to turn back. Yet another cable was made for the same ship, and in 1866 was laid successfully. Not only that, but the 1865 cable was recovered and spliced to one remaining on board; this provided two cables across the Atlantic. Part of the triumph could be ascribed to the Greenwich time signal which was received twice a day by the ship, making it possible to calculate its longitude accurately (see next chapter). The company's subsequent cable-laying ships would be moored off Greenwich.

The expansion of London Docks, in Britain's heyday as a world power, passed Greenwich by. Perhaps its roads and railways were not good enough to distribute the merchandise as it arrived from overseas. Furthermore, the City, with its merchants, and the East End, with its manufacturers, lay on the north side of the Thames. So when the Royal Dock was built in 1855 and the Royal Albert in 1880, they too were located on the north bank. Greenwich took note, launching its own bid for docks to be constructed on the peninsula in 1858 and 1881 – each time just a little too late, since the big new docks had already absorbed the demand. A Greenwich Dock would have dominated the area. Without it, the peninsula continued to support its brood of motley industries; and besides, though the big ships did not come into East Greenwich, their presence in such numbers just a short distance away provided all the more work for bargees and lightermen, and all the more call for Greenwich-built vessels to deliver cargoes from the Docks to elsewhere.

Not that the peninsula's industries were exclusively to do with ships, the river and the sea; far from it. The marsh, unseen and increasingly unsightly, was the place from which many appetites of the greedy behemoth of London, expanding rapidly, were supplied. There were brickworks, cementworks, works for making the creosote-soaked wood blocks that were used to pave many streets (Bethell's Timber Preserving Works became the Improved Wood Pavement Company). There was a company that crushed foreign seeds to extract oil (the London Seed Crushing Company). It went out of production in about 1900, just at the time that the Greenwich Inland Linoleum Company got underway. The latter was a big name in linoleum during the golden age of that floor covering; it ceased manufacture in 1935. There were businesses supplying ice, candles, soap, oxygen and animal feed. In 1867 a gun factory called the Blakeley Ordnance Works was built on the tip of the peninsula, where the Millennium Dome now stands, but it only lasted a few years. A rather more permanent presence was that of the South Metropolitan Gas Company, which converted mountains of coal, landed from the river from the big new screw-propeller-driven colliers, into the gas that flickered in the homes and streets of Victorian London. Its legacy of pollution caused the whole of the Millennium site to be sealed with a membrane before work on the Dome began.

Making coal gas and its by-product, tar, were not traditional river occupations, but, like many of the other activities on the peninsula, they depended upon the river for their supply of raw materials, and it was the existence of the river that determined their location. As though to emphasise the extent to which water was the natural element in these parts, there was even a station for the river police, on a floating pier.

* * *

Just at the time that Britain was celebrating its victory at Waterloo, a new and delightful method of reaching Greenwich made its appearance on the river. With a ring of the bell, a whistle of steam and perhaps a shower of soot, the first paddle-steamer whirred into motion. Soon the *Ariel*, the *Nymph*, the *Naiad*, the *Sylph* and the *Fairy* were all ploughing their cheerful way between Woolwich and Hungerford Bridge, stopping at Greenwich. Within a few years, another mode of travel was causing a sensation, as the first bout of railway mania convulsed Britain in the early 1820s. The earliest railways were in the north of England. In London, the travelling public may have been fascinated by them, but remained sceptical about their safety. The nervous had their worries about paddle-steamers, whose boilers had been known to explode. But the paddle-steamer, moving decorously along a river that had been sailed, if admittedly not paddled, for centuries, offered a rather less frightening experience to passengers than the steam locomotive running on iron rails.

The Kentish Railway Company was formed in 1824, with the object of opening a line from London to Greenwich and ultimately Dover, but the *Quarterly Review* would have none of it. It would be too expensive to build and too alarming to travel on. As it opined, in somewhat gusty style, in March 1825:

> It is certainly some consolation to those who are to be whirled at the rate of eighteen or twenty miles an hour, by means of a high pressure engine, to be told that they are in

no danger of being seasick while on shore; that they are not to be scalded to death, nor drowned by the bursting of the boiler; and that they need not fear being shot by the scattered fragments, or dashed to pieces by the flying off or the breaking of a wheel. But with all these assurances, we should as soon expect the people of Woolwich to suffer themselves to be fired off upon one of Congreve's ricochet rockets, as to trust themselves to the mercy of such a machine going at such a rate. Their property they may, perhaps, trust, but while one of the finest navigable rivers in the world runs parallel to the proposed railroad, we consider that the other twenty per cent which the subscribers are to receive for the conveyance of heavy goods is almost as problematical as that to be derived from the passengers. We will back old Father Thames against the Woolwich rail-way for any sum.

The Kentish Railway Company quietly expired.

Enter George Landmann and George Walter. Landmann had been born in Woolwich and brought up in Blackheath. Having served as a lieutenant-colonel with the Royal Engineers, he sold his army commission in 1824 and set himself up as a civil engineer. He formed a scheme for a line between London and Greenwich that would eventually run to Dover. Walter, though the son of a clergy-man, came from a family of financial risk-takers (one had lost a fortune in the South Sea Bubble). He had been in the navy, knew many people of influence, had experience of promoting railways and was a member of the stock exchange. Between them, Landmann and Walter had exactly the experience necessary to form a railway company. They did so in 1831, and called their proposed line the London and Greenwich Railway. It may have been under four miles in length, but it brought the railway to London.

Greenwich at that time had a population of 24,500 people. It had just been made a municipal borough. But it was still a separate entity from London. The wave of Georgian and Regency development, which created Gloucester Circus in Greenwich and the Paragon in Blackheath, had not caused this rock-pool to mingle its waters with those suburbs nearer the metropolis. There were still fields between the crowded little courts of Bermondsey and the now rather old-fashioned town of Deptford. The railway crossed country that was described, in 1835, as 'very rich ... almost wholly laid out in vegetable gardens'. The writer added prophetically: 'These will probably disappear ere long before the encroachments of brick and mortar.' There were wharfs along the riverfront at Greenwich, and the stirrings of industry on the marsh. The town itself, dominated by the Seamen's Hospital, was a contrast of large houses, with pretensions to gentility, and a jumble of odd little alleys around the river, next to the Seamen's Hospital, composed of ramshackle wooden buildings.

The Green Man at Greenwich was well known as the first stopping-place of the Dover Mail. The journey there, from Charing Cross, took at least an hour. For all that, a new horse omnibus service was started shortly before the railway came into prospect, its proprietor being the celebrated George Shillibeer. In 1834 Shillibeer gave up the other routes he had been running to concentrate all his twenty vehicles on the London-Greenwich-Woolwich run. It was popularly assumed that this would defeat the railway promoters. Safety was again uppermost in the public mind. The battle became the subject of a music-hall song entitled 'Shillibeer's Original Omnibus versus the Greenwich Railroad':

These pleasure and comfort with safety combine,
They will neither blow up nor explode like a mine;

Those who ride on the railroad might half die with fear,
You can come to no harm in the safe Shillibeer.

But the safe Shillibeer could not remain the prosperous Shillibeer, when battle was joined with the railway; before long he had gone out of business.

The railway strode down to Greenwich on arches – nearly a thousand of them. The viaduct, the purpose of which was to keep a steady gradient for the track, was a wonder in itself. 'As a work of art it is undoubtedly very striking, while the minor considerations involved in the plan are novel and interesting,' commented the *Penny Magazine* in January 1836. Even before the first trains were running, the company obtained a modest income from charging the public sixpence to walk down the line. It had been hoped that the arches could be turned into dwellings, and the *Penny Magazine* reported the optimistic verdict of a couple of families who were trying out two prototypes at Deptford.

One individual described the passing of a train, while he was within one of the houses, as resembling a distant roll of thunder, which was, however, from the rapidity of the motion, away in an instant; another thought it resembled the sudden passing of a heavily-laden waggon, the noise of which did not at all disturb his comfort. There will be different opinions upon this point, according to the varying sensitiveness of individuals, and no fair opportunity will be afforded of forming a correct judgment until the railway is opened and the traffic on it is begun. The noise will, however, be much less than many persons might be inclined to suppose; the solidity of the arches and the smoothness of the railway will diminish the vibration.

A better use was as storage or workshops: even at a time when the London slums were so overcrowded, the idea of living beneath railway arches did not take off.

The first experiments in running trains along sections of track took place in 1835, with the engineer Sir John Rennie, the Astronomer Royal, Professor Sir G. B. Airy, and the mathematician Charles Babbage being among the first passengers. Several Members of Parliament, the Swedish ambassador and the Prince of Orange joined the fashionable ladies making up parties to ride in the carriages. Not everyone was caught up in the enthusiasm, however. Sir Thomas Hardy, Nelson's old friend who was now governor of the Hospital, refused, on the grounds that it was pointless to take an unnecessary risk. And he may have felt vindicated when, on 12 November, the engine broke an axle on a new stretch of track and the train was derailed. The periodical *John Bull*, never a friend to the railways, was scathing:

> The loss of life upon the favourite toy from Liverpool to Manchester has already been terrific. Mr Huskisson was the first martyr to this favourite absurdity; and the last splendid exhibition took place only on Thursday, upon the new Tom-foolery to Greenwich, when in the outset 'by some accident', one of the carriages, in which a party of noodles ventured themselves, was thrown off the rail, but although it ran a vast many yards, no serious accident occurred. How lucky! Nobody killed the first day of trial!

'What have we let come amongst us?' asked a correspondent to a local Greenwich paper, under the signature of 'A Mourner', when the opening of the railway seemed imminent. 'This infernal Greenwich Railway, with all its thundering steam engines and omni*busters*, just ready to open, and destroy our rural town of Greenwich with red-hot cinders and hot water ...' But as the letter-writer admitted, it was too late to complain. In December 1836, with banners flying, bands playing national airs and the bells of parish churches pealing gaily, the first train to Deptford started – an hour and forty minutes late. The line reached Greenwich in 1838. The station was on the site of the present one. It is a short walk to the west of the town, opposite the almshouses founded by the Elizabethan antiquary William Lambarde.

And there it stopped. The intention had been simply to push onwards in a direct line towards Dover, but to do that would have meant crossing the Park. There was a proposal to run the railway on a viaduct between the Queen's House and the Observatory, an aesthetic disaster. It was not something that the people of Greenwich, not specially enamoured of the railway in the first place, would tolerate. Remarkably, in that age of expansion, the directors of the London and Greenwich accepted defeat. They turned to tunnelling instead. Professor Airy objected against the tunnel going under the Park, on the grounds that it would upset his instruments. So the directors adopted the more expensive option of tunnelling beneath the grounds of the Hospital; the result was called College Tunnel. It was not to be built for forty years. The sinking of the line was attended by the building of a new station, in 1878. By then it was too late to save East Greenwich's chances of becoming a major industrial centre: heavy ship-building now took place in the North. In view of Greenwich's subsequent development, as largely a residential suburb of London, this may have been just as well.

* * *

Elsewhere in Europe 1848 was the Year of Revolutions. This could hardly be said of Greenwich, but ten years after the railway first arrived, it was undeniably a different place from 1831, when the London and Greenwich Company was founded. The number of people living there had increased by five thousand, to just under thirty thousand inhabitants. The Hospital had introduced various schemes to improve the character of the town, and the building of the new market in 1831 entailed sweeping away some of the worst streets. The old wooden houses were being replaced by brick façades: often no more than façades applied to old structures. With their smart shop fronts, they were transforming Church Street into a place of regularity and order. It was still an age of small specialist shops. There were no fewer than twenty-seven straw-hat makers, twenty-two cowkeepers, seventy-seven hotels, inns and taverns, fifty-six beer-houses and, just as surprisingly, twenty-six surgeons and three physicians. Gas was provided by the Phoenix Gas Company, which had been supplying the town – or that section which could afford it – from six gasometers in Bridge Street since 1827. The main streets were now lit by gas.

Concerts were held (the librarian was sacked for attempting to charge 10 per cent on admissions), and the East Greenwich Madrigal Society met weekly at the Mitre. A Literary Institute had opened in 1837, followed by the Greenwich Society for the Diffusion of Useful Knowledge in 1843. The Temperance Society met monthly and, if we can believe its own verdict, 'accomplished much in ameliorating the condition and elevating the character of some of the most degraded of our fellow countrymen'. The town was overrun with places of worship: two congregational churches, a Baptist chapel, a Wesleyan Methodist chapel, and an English Presbyterian church and the Catholic Our Lady Star of the Sea both rising – all in addition to the Church of England's St Alfege's and St

Pastoral Greenwich, photographed on 11 August 1858. The view shows Woodlands home farm, Combe Farm and Greenwich Marshes, with the masts of ships on the Thames visible in the distance.

Mary's. For all the front of respectability, there was a seditious undercurrent, with Chartists meeting secretly in their Wat Tyler Club and rallying on Blackheath. The large number of foreigners, who came with the ships and sometimes made Greenwich their home, added a note of colour. In the previous century a society of anti-Gallicans met at the Chocolate House on Blackheath, presumably in response to the many French people living in the area.

'Situated on the banks of a noble river, and adjacent to a beautiful park; the salubrious air, and the charming views from the hills and the high grounds in and around it, render it a delightful place of resort for all classes.' Such was the judgement of *The Stranger's Guide to Greenwich* of 1855. It is no wonder, then, that its population grew and grew, to 46,500 in 1881. This led W. Howarth, author of *Greenwich: Past and Present* of 1885, to comment: 'Perhaps never before have houses been erected to such a great extent as in the last ten or fifteen years. *East* Greenwich, as we term it, has lately felt the hand of change upon it; the fields and meadow lands of a short time ago are now streets of thickly populated houses.'

Such was the reality of Greenwich towards the end of the nineteenth century: an active, developing suburb, with more than its fair share, one would imagine, of awkward, argumentative people, commercially minded and church-going, their English solidity spiced with a sprinkling of foreigners and a tang of the sea. But as the name of Greenwich flew around the world it was associated, not with a tangible, durable and populous neighbourhood beside the Thames, but with that most ethereal and fleeting of concepts – Time.

THE WORLD
SETS ITS WATCH

I N 1833, a curious ritual could be observed at the Royal
Observatory. A tall spike supporting a weathervane had been
erected on top of one of the turrets. It had been made by
Messrs Maudslay, Son and Field (still of Lambeth: they had not yet
acquired the National Company for Boat Building by Machinery on
Greenwich Marsh) who also constructed, out of sight, a winding
apparatus on the floor below the turret. At five minutes to one, a
big red ball was hoisted halfway up the spike. At two minutes to
one, it rose as far as it could, to the crossbars of the weathervane. At
one o'clock exactly, it came plummeting down again. This is said to
have been the world's first public time signal. The ball could plainly
be seen from the river, and the mariners whose vessels were about
to sail down the Thames, out into the estuary and perhaps to far-
flung places around the world, knew that it would begin to fall at
precisely one o'clock. They could set their watches by it.

Time had been a preoccupation of astronomers working in the
Royal Observatory since it was founded. Without an accurate idea of
what time it was, seafarers were unable to plot their longitudinal position at sea. By the nineteenth century, they had the chronometers that
could enable them to do this. But these timepieces, to be accurate,
needed to be set to the correct time in the first place. It was difficult, if
not impossible, to make the precise lunar observations that would give
the time while a ship was at sea. This could be done ashore, but was

not very convenient. An observatory clock could be used to adjust a pocket watch, which was then carried to the chronometer on board ship (the chronometer itself was too sensitive to move). This was cumbersome. In short, no method was perfect. Sometimes ships at sea were alerted by means of guns or rockets fired, or flags dipped, but these were not regular occurrences. As an experiment, a timeball was erected at the entrance to Portsmouth Harbour in 1829; and in 1833 Captain Robert Wauchope of the Royal Navy, the champion of the timeball, suggested to the Admiralty that one should be set up at Greenwich. John Pond, the Astronomer Royal, was quick to agree. On 28 October, the Lords Commissioners of the Admiralty gave notice that a timeball 'will henceforward be dropped ... By observing the first instant to its downward movement, all vessels in the adjacent reaches of the river as well as in most of the docks, will thereby have an opportunity of regulating and rating their chronometers.' Noon might have seemed a more obvious time to choose than one o'clock; but noon was the moment when the astronomers were making the observations to find the time in the first place.

Soon, however, it would not only be mariners who wanted to keep the exact time. Following the railway's arrival in Greenwich in 1838, by the middle of the century, the whole of the country had been cross-hatched with iron lines. The guards waving off the trains would look importantly at their official timepieces, to keep the service running precisely to time. But whose time was it? Because of the curvature of the earth's surface, the sun rises and sets at a slightly different time in each part of Britain. Before the railways, time did not have the same importance that it was to assume in a busier age. There were few public clocks, and not all of them were accurate. Those that were carefully regulated – the clocks on town halls, for example – were set to local time. The local time in Bristol, to the west of London, was sixteen minutes behind that of the capital.

That did not matter when those places were a world away from each other. But once they had been joined by the railway, and not only joined to each other but to dozens of other towns and cities, so that the possibilities of the system became more and more complex, there was no room for local variations in time. Fortunately, just as the railways provided the need for a standard time, they also provided them with the means by which it could be distributed.

The idea of introducing a standard time throughout Britain was not absolutely new. It had been advocated by one of the Commissioners for Longitude, Captain Basil Hall, as well as Abraham Follett Osler. According to a report of a lecture given by Osler to the Birmingham Philosophical Institution, which appeared in the very first issue of the *Illustrated London News* (14 May 1842), Osler urged it upon the Postmaster General, Rowland Hill, 'as a matter of some importance in connection with the post-office department'. Neither Hall nor Osler was the first to come up with the notion of standard Post Office time; he ascribed the credit for that to Dr William Hyde Wollaston, who died as early as 1828. Hyde proposed that all post-office clocks throughout the United Kingdom should be regulated 'by means of the time brought from London by the mail-coach chronometers; and he had no doubt that, ere long, all the town clocks, and, eventually, all the clocks and watches of private persons, would fall into the same course of regulation; so that only one expression of time would prevail over the country, and every clock and watch indicate by its hands the same hour and minute at the same moment of absolute time'. For this purpose, time was like any other commodity, to be distributed around the country physically. The idea was sound but there was as yet no urgent reason to adopt it. The means of implementation – carrying clocks around the country by coach – may seem impractical; yet that was pretty much how time was delivered to chronometer makers around

London until the 1930s. Miss Ruth Belville, the daughter of one of the Observatory assistants, visited the Observatory every Monday, checked her personal timepiece (a 'warming pan' of a silver watch made by John Arnold and Son), then made the rounds of the major clock-makers in London.

Parliament was slow on the uptake: it rejected petitions for introducing a standard time. But the railways had to get on with

The Astronomer Royal, Sir George Airy, championed the sending-out of time signals from the Observatory. Here *Punch* has caricatured him in 1883 as the Greenwich timeball.

it. In 1840 the Great Western Railway ordered that London time would apply throughout its network, and one after another the other railway companies followed suit. The Post Office fell in with them. Before long, the public clocks in major provincial cities such as Manchester showed London time. This was not, strictly speaking, Greenwich time, but the body co-ordinating railway operations between the companies officially adopted Greenwich time in 1847. It was therefore in place before the Great Exhibition of 1851 caused an enormous movement of people around the country, with some six million people making the journey to Crystal Palace, the vast majority of them by train.

The Astronomer Royal, George Airy, believed that it was the 'very proper duty of the National Observatory to promote by utilitarian aid the dissemination of a knowledge of accurate time which is now really a matter of very great importance'. Fortunately, just as demand was arising for a standard time throughout Britain, science provided a method by which a signal could be sent instantaneously to any part of the kingdom, and the railways were supplying the wires along which it would be transmitted. Electricity (or, as it was then known, galvanism) could be used to regulate all the clocks throughout the Observatory. More than that, as Airy reported to his Board of Visitors in June 1849:

The same means will probably by employed to increase the general utility of the Observatory, by the extensive dissemination throughout the Kingdom of accurate time-signals, moved by an original clock at the Royal Observatory; and I have already entered into correspondence with the authorities of the South Eastern Railway (whose line of galvanic communication will shortly pass within nine furlongs of the Observatory) in reference to this subject ...

Telegraph lines were laid from the Observatory to Lewisham station in 1852. From Lewisham the signal would flash to London Bridge station, and from there around the other stations of the South Eastern Railway. More importantly, it went also to the distribution centre of the Electric Telegraph Company in the City of London; this was connected with offices all over the country. Since 1851 there had even been a cable beneath the English Channel, so that Greenwich time could be bestowed on the Continent. It was not without mechanical difficulties. The underground wire to Lewisham failed in 1859, so overhead wires were constructed to the Electric Telegraph Company. Other wires were constructed to Greenwich station, for the benefit of the South Eastern Railway; this signal operated a timeball – one of half a dozen hoisted around the country – at Deal, in Kent. To Airy, reviewing the achievement in 1865, it was a blessing that Britain enjoyed above other countries. 'The practical result of the system will be acknowledged by all those who have travelled abroad. We can, on an English railway, always obtain correct time, but not so on a French or German railway, where the clocks are often found considerably in error.' Oh, the hopelessness of foreigners, to the Victorian mind!

But there was one respect in which the British way was less than perfect. While the whole of the country operated according to Greenwich time, the legal system did not recognise it. In theory, this could have serious consequences: there might be confusion as to, say, whether an insurance policy was in effect if a man died close to midnight. As it turned out, the muddle seems to have been restricted to different parties in court cases arriving at different times (Greenwich and local), and pedantic officials being uncertain when officially to open and close polling booths during general elections. The anomaly was put right by Act of Parliament in 1880, when Greenwich time was adopted for purposes of law.

So much for Britain. But time knows no national boundaries; ships pass from one national jurisdiction to another; even before the age of radio and telephone it was recognised that for different countries to keep different times was inconvenient. Since 1870 scientists and geographers had been bending their minds towards the question of a prime meridian: that is, a line of longitude which everyone acknowledged as zero. Early astronomers, from the Ancients onwards, took their observatories as the meridian. Thus for Hipparchos, the first astronomer to perceive longitude, it was Rhodes. To early royal astronomers in France, it was Paris. But the prime meridian that was most widely used happened to be Greenwich. The explanation for this lies in the British *Nautical Almanac* first published in 1767. This supplied the information from which seafarers of all nations calculated their positions. And from the late eighteenth century Greenwich came to be taken as zero longitude on many maps and charts, whether or not they originated in Britain. These included J. F. W. DesBarres's 'Atlantic Neptune' covering the east coast of North America from Labrador to the Gulf of Mexico. Most American charts for the next half-century were based on DesBarres, entrenching the Greenwich meridian in the New World.

A move to adopt the Greenwich meridian as the prime meridian of the world was made at the first International Geographical Congress, which took place in Antwerp in 1871. Three years later, an International Meridian Conference was convened at Washington. The Canadian geographer Sanford Fleming produced figures on the extent to which shipping followed the different meridians then current. He calculated that the Greenwich meridian 'is used by 72 per cent of the whole floating commerce of the world, while the remaining 28 per cent is divided among ten different initial meridians'. Not everyone agreed that there should be a prime meridian (an unexpected dissenter was Airy, so progressive in establishing a common time), or that the meridian adopted ought to be Greenwich. Some thought it should be based on an island, such as the Azores; or on a mountain, like Tenerife; in a strait, like the Baring Strait; or on some timeless historical monument, such as the Great Pyramid or Temple of Jerusalem. After that were the observatories of Paris, Berlin and Washington. In a masterly, though unsuccessful, negotiation, the French said they would accept Greenwich as the prime meridian only if Great Britain adopted the metric system. The Conference overrode the French objections. They recommended to the different governments from which the delegates came that Greenwich should become the prime meridian. Another resolution proposed that this new, universally recognised zero longitude should also be the legally recognised date line for the world. So it is at Greenwich, at midnight, that one day officially turns into the next. With the exception of New Zealand, every country in the world will take the start of the new millennium as 00h 00m 00s Universal Time (within 0.9 of a second of Greenwich Mean Time). In other words, the millennium begins at Greenwich.

It took a little longer for time around the world to be co-ordinated according to Greenwich Time. But it happened sure enough. With international telegraphy and the radio, a standard time was inevitable. Serbia 1884; Japan 1888; Belgium, Holland, South Africa 1892; Italy, Germany, Austria-Hungary 1893 ... so it went on. Only France continued stubbornly to go its own way, adopting Paris Mean Time as *l'heure nationale* by a law of 1891. Five years later, there was an attempt to persuade the *Chambre des Députés* to substitute Greenwich Mean Time. *Greenwich* Time? That was a little too strong for the patriotic deputies, who proposed that the time adopted should in fact be Paris Mean Time diminished by nine minutes twenty-one seconds (Greenwich Time without the Greenwich). This went up to the Senate, who passed it to a commission. It was only in 1911 that the bill was enacted. That law stayed on the statute book until 1978 when France adopted Universal Time.

Universal Time is co-ordinated from Paris. But it is based not on Paris Time but on Greenwich Time. The discrepancy of nearly a second from Greenwich Time is explained by the development of quartz and atomic clocks, which are more reliable than the globe itself. It is now known that the world does not rotate at an *absolutely* constant speed, and there is an infinitesimal wobble in its orbit. For all that, the prime meridian on which the world's time is based is still that which passes through Greenwich.

The Millennium
Comes in with a Roar

S OME TIME IN THE MID-1890S, William Bull, a London
county councillor, visited the Blackwall Tunnel, whose path
was then being driven through the alternately sandy, grav-
elly and clay-y soils that form the Thames basin. The tunnel would
connect East Greenwich, on the south bank of the Thames, with
the Isle of Dogs, on the north. The digging of it had been talked
about for decades. There were no bridges across the Thames below
Tower Bridge: they would have impeded shipping. But the geology
of the river bed made tunnelling too dangerous. The slippery soils
threatened to collapse upon the work.

Recently, however, a technique for boring through difficult
conditions had been pioneered in New York. It involved the use of
compressed air: effectively, the tunnel was inflated until its sides
could be secured against the outside pressure. Dozens of people
died in the effort to complete the Hudson River tunnel, until the
British contractor Sir Weetman Pearson found a means to counter-
act caissons disease – a condition equivalent to the bends suffered
by deep sea divers. Pearson brought his experience to bear on the
Blackwall project. In the end, not one of the workmen lost his life.

Nevertheless, Councillor Bull may well have thought that his
journey into the depths of the tunnel would be a descent into the
unknown. He was certainly conscious of the heroic scale of the

enterprise. 'This is a gigantic undertaking,' he wrote, 'one of the greatest during the latter part of this century.'

To gain admission to the construction site, Councillor Bull and his party had to enter an air lock. The doors were like those of a safe. Compressed air was forced into the chamber and people began to worry that they could no longer breathe. Some found that their ears and noses bled. Then the low buzzing noise of the air pump ceased. The required pressure had been achieved, and the iron door that led to the drill head, being driven forward by twenty-eight hydraulic rams, swung open. Councillor Bull's description of the atmosphere is graphic:

> You can scarcely hear each other speak at first. John Burns' deep voice has a far-off sound as if he were a furlong away. Our cigars burn with the rapidity of cigarettes, and if a champagne bottle were opened it would go off without a pop. We are living at double our normal rate! Air is being pumped in at the rate of six thousand cubic feet per minute by four powerful engines, and two more are always kept in readiness with steam up to increase the supply. This amount of oxygen gives one a curious hilarity or lightness of spirit, and one would whistle if one could – but that is exactly what you cannot do.

Councillor Bull wanted to inspect every part of this miraculous tunnel. Summoning his courage, he poked around the bulwarks at the cutting edge, beside a huge drill that had been put out of action through hitting a huge piece of fossilised rock. 'I feel very cold about the ankles,' he remarked to his guide.'Yes, that is the water rising,' he was told coolly. 'The pumps have stopped working for a minute, but they will get it under before it reaches your waist.'

It says something for the industrial activity that the nineteenth century had brought to life on Greenwich Marsh that it should have been chosen for the southern entrance to the tunnel. The tunnel itself reflects the faith that Greenwich has always had in the future. It seems appropriate that the tunnel's air vents are clearly visible in the Millennium Dome, the only pre-existing element on the site to have actively shaped this most forward-looking architectural endeavour. The engineers who built the tunnel would have rejoiced to see the Dome rise. They would have known the site of the Dome as a gasworks – reputed to be the largest in England.

To construct the Dome, the land contaminated by the gasworks had to be cleared and cleansed; plans made; planning permission obtained; sponsors sought; and the resources of the latest technology marshalled so that the whole project would be completed, down to the last detail, within the staggeringly short period of five years.

With his grizzled beard, the Dome's architect Michael Davies of Richard Rogers Associates, might almost be thought to resemble the Victorian entrepreneurs whose spirit he seems to revive – except that the beard is balanced by a pony-tail, and the monochrome in which he dresses is not Victorian black but fire-engine red. (Red shirt, red trousers, red shoes, red construction hat, red mobile phone: no one could accuse him of inconsistency.)

The Dome is a rich source of statistics for Mr Davies. No one has ever driven a golf ball further than the diameter of the Dome. You could lay the Eiffel Tower down in it and its feet would not stick out. The circumference is the exact size of the Avebury Ring. Construction workers, chosen for their skills in abseiling, had to move along swathes of fabric as big as a ski slope – 'just like Val d'Isère,' as Davies put it.

To equip the Dome with its contents has been just as much of a challenge as building it. 'It was like climbing a mountain,' says Jenny Page, chief executive of the Millennium Experience Company which controlled this great enterprise, 'with only a short time to do it before the snows came down.' The project's guiding light, she continued, was a saying of the French political philosopher Alexis de Tocqueville. He divided nations into those that are hoping to rise and those that are fearing to fall. A nation that builds a Millennium Dome still has a bit of energy about it. Or, as a French politician is supposed to have remarked to one of the progenitors of the Dome, 'We are meant to be the ones who do this sort of thing, not you.'

The optimism that is so manifest in the Dome radiates throughout the whole of Greenwich. This is all the more remarkable, given that the twentieth century was not universally kind to the Borough. The opening of the twentieth century saw Greenwich in a dirty and depressed state. Industry had got the upper hand. Gentility had largely fled, and with it the shades of the kings and queens, courtiers, sea captains and members of the Royal Society who had in previous ages built houses here. Even Gloucester Circus, which had looked so dashing when it had been built a hundred years before, was now a series of shabby tenements, whose occupants worked in East Greenwich or the Docks on the other side of the river. Horse-drawn vehicles could squeeze onto the somewhat narrow carriageways of the Blackwall Tunnel. Pedestrians could also use the foot tunnel built by the London County Council in 1902, its southern entrance now adjacent to the Cutty Sark. It replaced the old ferry.

Proximity to the Docks was no blessing during the Second World War: Greenwich suffered heavily from bombing. By the river the Ship Tavern was reduced to rubble. The bright smile of the Paragon on Blackheath lost four of its teeth, two pairs of houses being blown out by either the Luftwaffe or flying bombs. Hawksmoor's St Alfege's church was burnt out. On the other hand, Greenwich had escaped the worst of the suburban development taking place around London before the War. The town hall, in the

View of the Isle of Dogs and (bottom right) Greenwich, 1940, taken from a German bomber. Many bombs intended for more important targets instead hit such monuments as St Alfege's church, the Paragon and the Ship tavern.

Dutch Dudok style, could have been worse. Generally Greenwich entered the 1950s shabby but – bomb damage apart – intact.

Since then, Greenwich has been setting its sails towards a new destiny. A symbol of this endeavour is the *Cutty Sark*. It is now such an inseparable part of the Greenwich scene that it takes some effort of imagination to think of the time before the ship came to its home next to the Greenwich landing stage. Its rescue dates from the years immediately after the Second World War, when decisions had to be taken about the last of the wooden vessels to survive from Britain's nineteenth-century maritime supremacy. One December day in 1949 *HMS Implacable*, which had fought at Trafalgar, was blown up off the south coast. This made people who loved old ships determined to prevent the like happening again. The *Cutty Sark* first arrived at Greenwich as part of the Festival of Britain celebrations in 1951, and the Duke of Edinburgh was prominent in the campaign to have her permanently docked there. This object was achieved in 1954. As the *Cutty Sark*'s rigging rose beside the Thames, Greenwich itself seemed to recapture some of its old confidence and identity.

The focus of the new Greenwich, so to speak, has been the National Maritime Museum, occupying Inigo Jones's Queen's House and its nineteenth-century wings. The Museum is no johnny-come-lately in the history of Greenwich. From the time of Nelson's funeral, the Seamen's Hospital contained relics of naval interest. The Painted Hall, almost from the moment of its creation, ceased to fulfil its original purpose as a dining-room, serving instead as a national achievement that could be shown to visitors. Pensioners collected useful amounts of money for the Hospital – as well as emoluments for themselves – by acting as guides. Athenian Stuart's new chapel provided another attraction. By the mid-1790s, when the wars on the Continent gave domestic tourism a fillip, the Hospital was taking over £570 a year from visitors. George IV gave thirty portraits of naval commanders to the Seamen's Hospital to augment, very substantially, the modest number of paintings that it possessed, and the Painted Hall was turned into a gallery – the National Gallery of Naval Art – to show them. It formed the basis of the Royal Naval Museum, established at Greenwich Hospital in 1873.

In time the Royal Naval Museum evolved into the National Maritime Museum, which opened in 1937. Perhaps appropriately, the opening day inspired a recrudescence of the boisterous behaviour associated with Greenwich Fair: despite free entry, some of the five thousand people who visited the Museum climbed over the railings, all the soap and towels in the lavatories were pocketed and men used the fireplaces in the Queen's House to urinate. It would not have happened in the National Gallery, the Victoria and Albert Museum or the Science Museum; somehow Greenwich, and the public it attracted, were different.

Soon Britain was at war. Inevitably, therefore, it was the naval aspect of 'Maritime' which dominated the Museum's early life. But it also participated in the surge of national redefinition associated with the Festival of Britain (under a Labour government) in 1951 and the Coronation of Queen Elizabeth II (under the Conservatives) two years later. When the Royal Observatory, finding that the skies of London were too polluted for observations still to be made from Greenwich, moved its telescopes to Herstmonceux Castle in Sussex in 1948, the National Maritime Museum assumed responsibility for the old building. Flamsteed House and the Octagon Room opened to the public shortly after the Festival of Britain. In 1951 Her Majesty the Queen opened the East Wing of the Museum.

Recently money from the National Lottery has made it possible to remove what was originally a gymnasium (surviving from the time when the Queen's House was occupied by the Royal Hospital School) and develop the Neptune Court. This provides some twenty new galleries and display spaces. In addition, the status of the old Royal Observatory is set to develop. In the future, it will not only continue to be a museum which the public can visit to experience something of the past history of astronomical endeavour: it will be charged with interpreting the present state of man's knowledge of the cosmos to the public. There is exciting talk of a simultaneous video link with a proposed new telescope in Hawaii, which could be operated remotely from Greenwich: since the skies over Hawaii would be dark during what is daytime for Greenwich, this would enable visitors to explore the heavens for themselves.

There is a brave new future for buildings of the Seamen's Hospital, otherwise the Royal Naval College, too. Three centuries of occupation by the Royal Navy have ended. In the process was revealed one of the unexpected and somewhat unwelcome layers of Greenwich history – the existence of a nuclear reactor on the site. The reactor (endearingly known as Jason) was installed by the Royal Naval College to give officers the opportunity to study nuclear power as related to submarines. The Ministry of Defence failed to take its existence into account when planning the navy's retreat from Greenwich, which as a result took longer than originally expected. But now Wren's colonnades shelter the University of Greenwich. The cultural significance both of this complex and the Park has been recognised by UNESCO, who have declared Greenwich to be a World Heritage Site.

Now the Dome has arisen as the latest in the long line of architectural excitements in Greenwich. The Dome, naturally, has a significance that goes beyond the context in which it sits. As the focus of a great national celebration, it can hardly fail to be taken as a paradigm of the British character. But Greenwich, too, has something to teach us about ourselves, our place in the world and in the twenty-first century. National character is not formed in one burst of fireworks, but through the shared experience of centuries. In Greenwich, that shared experience includes strands which we would do well to carry with us into the future. The story of Greenwich, as we have seen, contains its fair share of pomp, extravagance, cruelty, militarism, suffering and inequality. It is a story of struggle, as some factions rise and others fall. But set within this drama are scenes of greater human worth. History marks Greenwich as outward-looking, adventurous, inventive, inclusive and humanitarian: these are qualities on which the new British identity being forged at this time of change can be founded. Let us bring to mind the holiday crowds tumbling down the Giant's Steps, the many charities founded here, the civic spirit expressed in the architecture, the casual bravery of the sailors who left Greenwich in the fishing fleet, the environmentalism of what Saxons called the Green Market.

With its new museum galleries, its Millennium Dome, its Jubilee Line station in East Greenwich and its promised Docklands Light Railway station in the historic centre, Greenwich is as up-to-the-minute as anywhere. Yet its ability to keep pace with the future has not been at the expense of its great past. The age of the automobile, now waning, may not, in all respects, have treated Greenwich kindly. But it has survived into an era in which the motor car will be less dominant with its human scale and green spaces intact. Now that transport priorities are changing and improved quality of life has become a universal goal, Greenwich has every reason to celebrate. This rather quiet place by the Thames, settled for a millennium or more, brings the next millennium in with a roar.

FURTHER READING

By far the richest source of material on Greenwich is Edward Hasted's *Hundred of Blackheath*, a history based on two manuscript collections, and in turn edited by Henry H. Drake, 1886. It is a cornucopia of references, but in the manner of cornucopias, the organising principle appears to be rich profusion rather than conventional orderliness. An enormous amount is contained in it if you look. Contemporary sources for which I give no other reference will generally be found in Hasted. The antiquarian background is painted in the three Kent volumes of the *Victoria County History*, 1908, 1926 and 1932. A synopsis of Greenwich's architectural monuments is provided by the *London South* volume of Bridget Cherry and Nikolaus Pevsner's *Buildings of England*, 1983. H. M. Colvin's *Biographical Dictionary of British Architects* is the first place to search for information on any Greenwich (or other) architect. The building of Bella Court, Placentia, the Queen's House and Charles II's palace can be traced in the first five volumes of H. M. Colvin (ed), *The History of the King's Works*, 1963, 1975 and 1976. There have been a number of general books about Greenwich over the years. In the same year that Hasted's monumental volume appeared, 1886, A. G. L'Estrange's *The Palace and the Hospital, or Chronicles of Greenwich* was published. More recently, Olive and Neil Hamilton produced their illustrated *Royal Greenwich* (Greenwich, 1969). Beryl Platts's *A History of Greenwich*, Newton Abbot, 1973, provides a narrative history, particularly strong on the early centuries, if sometimes touched by romanticism. Felix Barker's admirable *Greenwich and Blackheath Past*, with pictures accompanying a rather spare text, came out in 1993. The history of Blackheath is comprehensively detailed in *Blackheath Village and Environs, 1790–1990*, 2 vols, Blackheath, 1976 and 1983, by Neil Rhind. Many papers on Greenwich history have been published in the *Transactions of the Greenwich and Lewisham Antiquarian Society* since the beginning of the twentieth century. The Society and its *Transactions* still flourish. Beyond that, the best starting point for research on Greenwich is the subject catalogue of the Society of Antiquaries, with its many references to topographical works in the Society's collections. Moreover, Greenwich is blessed with a first-rate local history library in what used to be the Angerstein country house of Woodlands, in Mycenae Road.

PRINCIPAL SOURCES

(All books published in London unless otherwise stated.)

PROLOGUE

Fairburn's Edition of the Funeral of Admiral Lord Nelson, 1806. *A Complete Account of the Procession and Ceremony Observed at the Funeral of Lord Nelson, Thursday, January 9, 1806* (reprinted Eugene, Oregon, 1991).

The Times and the *Naval Chronicle* for 1805 and 1806.

Frederick Locker-Lampson, *My Confidences*, 1896.

A DEAD STICK BURSTS INTO LEAF

National Sites and Monuments Record, Greater London (computerised record of archaeological finds), kept by English Heritage, London Division.

Reg Rigden, *The Romans in the Greenwich District*, Greenwich, 1974.

Harvey Sheldon and Brian Yule, 'Excavations in Greenwich Park, 1978–79', reprinted from the *London Archaeologist*, 1979.

Arthur D. Sharp, 'St Alfege', *Transactions of the Greenwich and Lewisham Antiquarian Society*, vol.4, 1936, pp 6–16.

Britannia Sancta: or, the Lives of the Most Celebrated British, English, Scottish and Irish Saints, 1745.

N. A. M. Rodger, *The Safeguard of the Sea: A Naval History of Britain, 600–1612*, 1997.

Kerry Downes, *Hawksmoor*, 1959.

H. M. Colvin, 'Fifty New Churches', *Architectural Review*, March 1950.

RCHME, *Greenwich Park, An Archaeological Survey*, 1994.

LA MAISON DE GRENEVWYC

Beryl Platts, op. cit.

K. H. Vickers, *Humphrey Duke of Gloucester*, 1907.

Hasted, op. cit.

G. Kriehn, *The English Rising of 1450*, 1892.

Mary Clive, *This Sun of York*, 1973.

Simon Thurley in *The Royal Palaces of Tudor England*, 1993.

IF YOU ARE THE DAUPHIN OF FRANCE, I WISH TO KISS YOU

Van Cleave Alexander, *The First of the Tudors*, 1981.

Thurley, op. cit.

An English translation of the letters from the Venetian embassy can be found at the Public Record Office, Kew (*The Calendars of the State Papers: Venetian*, 19 vols). It is presented as a calendar; that is to say, a précis of the original documents, though sometimes the translation appears to be direct (I have quoted it as such in the text). Extracts from the papers are quoted in John M. Stone, 'Greenwich History as Told by Venetian Records', *Transactions of the Greenwich and Lewisham Antiquarian Society*, c. 1912.

Philip Dixon, *Excavations at Greenwich Palace, 1970–71*, 1971.

Francis Henry Cripps-Day, *Fragmenta Armamentaria*, vol. 1, part II, 'An Introduction to the Study of Greenwich Armour'.

M. Oppenheim, *A History of the Administration of the Royal Navy*, 1896.

N. A. M. Rodger, op. cit.

John Gough Nichols (ed), *Literary Remains of King Edward the Sixth*, vol. 2.

J. W. Kirby, 'Alfonso Ferrabosco of Greenwich (1573?–1627) Court Musician', *Transactions of the Greenwich and Lewisham Antiquarian Society*, vol. 3, 1924–34, pp. 207–17.

John Kimbell, *An Account of the legacies, gifts and charities for Church and Poor, in the Parish of St Alphege, Greenwich*, Greenwich, 1816.

LOVE AND KINDNESS INCREASE DAILY BETWEEN THEM

John Summerson, *Inigo Jones*, 1966.

John Harris and Gordon Higgott, *Inigo Jones, Complete Architectural Drawings* (Royal Academy exhibition catalogue), February 1990.

G. H. Chettle in *The Queen's House. Greenwich*, a London Survey Committee monograph, 1937.

J. Charlton, *The Queen's House*, 1976.

Stephen Orgen and Roy Strong's monumental *Inigo Jones, the Theatre of the Stuart Court*, 2 vols, 1973.

G. P. V. Akrigg, *Jacobean Pageant or the Court of King James I*, 1962.

G. P. V, Akrigg, *Letters of King James VI and I*, 1984.

Anne Somerset, *Unnatural Murder*, 1997.

The Calendars of the State Papers: Venetian, op. cit.

N. E. McClure (ed), *The Letters of John Chamberlain*, 2 vols, Philadelphia, 1939.

Carola Oman, *Henrietta Maria*, 1951.

I HAVE NEVER LIVED SO MERRILY AS I HAVE DONE THIS PLAGUE-TIME

W. H. Mandy, 'Notes from the Assize Rolls and Other Documents Relating to the Hundred of Blackheath', *Transactions of the Greenwich and Lewisham Antiquarian Society*, vol. 1, 1913, pp. 300–2.

Jane Burkitt, 'Greenwich at the End of the 17th Century', *Transactions of the Greenwich and Lewisham Antiquarian Society*, vol. 8, 1977 (published 1978), pp. 223–33.

John Bold, *John Webb*, Oxford.

Derek Howse, *Francis Place and the Early History of the Greenwich Observatory*, Oxford, 1989.

Richard Ollard, *Pepys*, 1974 (illustrated edition 1990).

R. C. Latham and W. Matthews, *The Diary of Samuel Pepys*, 9 vols, from 1971.

John Summerson, *Sir Christopher Wren*, 1953.

Kerry Downes, *Christopher Wren*, 1971. Wren's buildings, with documents, have all been published in the 20 vols of the Wren Society; the Royal Observatory features in vol. 19, pp. 113–15.

Derek Howse, *Greenwich Time and the Longitude*, 1997 (first published 1980 as *Greenwich Time and the Discovery of the Longitude*).

F. Baily, *An Account of the Rev'd John Flamsteed, the First Astronomer Royal*, 1835.

Eric G. Forbes, Lesley Murdin and Frances Willmoth (eds), *The Correspondence of John Flamsteed, the First Astronomer Royal*, 2 vols, Bristol, 1995 and 1997.

Wren and London's estimate of damages was published in *Notes and Queries*, 10 May 1856.

LAST LIGHT ON THE WAVE OF TIME

Jock Haswell, *James II: Soldier, Sailor*, 1972.

Pieter van der Merwe, *'A Refuge for All'. Greenwich Hospital, 1694–1994*, Greenwich, 1994.

John Cooke and John Maule, *An Historical Account of the Royal Hospital for Seamen at Greenwich*, 1789.

Edward Fraser, *Greenwich Hospital and the Royal United Services Museum*, 1910.

Philip Newell, *Greenwich Hospital. A Royal Foundation, 1692–1983*, 1984.

The hospital's architecture is the subject of vol. 6 of the Wren Society. We await what will no doubt prove the definitive study, the Survey of London volume edited by John Bold.

David Watkin, *Athenian Stuart, Pioneer of the Greek Revival*, 1982.

Lesley Lewis, 'The Architects of the Chapel at Greenwich Hospital', *Art Bulletin*, vol. 29–30 (1947–8), pp. 260–7.

Jeanne-Marie Philipon Roland, 'A Trip to England', in *The Works ... of Jeanne-Marie Philipon Roland*, translated from the French, 1800.

Clare Williams (ed and trans), *Sophie in London, 1786, being the Diary of Sophie von la Roche*, 1933.

The diary of the First Earl of Egremont is published in vol. 63 of the Historical Manuscript Commission Reports, kept in the British Library.

SIR JOHN VANBRUGH PLAYS AT CASTLES

Kerry Downes, op. cit.

Kerry Downes, 'The Little Colony on Greenwich Hill', *Country Life*, 27 May 1976, pp. l406–8.

Neil Rhind, *Blackheath Village and Environs, 1790–1970*, vol. 2, Blackheath, 1983.

H. G. Lovegrove, *London Topographical Record*, iv, 1907.

Laurence Whistler, *The Imagination of Vanbrugh and his Fellow Artists*, 1954, pp. 200–6.

W. E. L. Fletcher, 'The Maze Hill Estate of Sir John Vanbrugh', *Transactions of the Greenwich and Lewisham Antiquarian Society*, vol. 8, 1978, pp. 136–42.

AS MUCH DELIGHT AND HONOUR AS THIS WORLD CAN GIVE

Neil Rhind, *The Heath*, Blackheath, 1987.

Daniel Defoe, *Tour Through England and Wales*, 1724–6.

Derek Howse, *Francis Place*, op. cit.

Lord Egremont, op. cit.

Cyril Fry, 'The Angersteins of Woodlands', *Transactions of the Greenwich and Lewisham Antiquarian Society*, vol. 7, 1964–72.

Neil Rhind, op. cit.

Charles Alister, 'Montague House, Blackheath', *Transactions of the Greenwich and Lewisham Antiquarian Society*, vol. 8, 1973–8.

Francis Bickley (ed), *The Diaries of Sylvester Douglas (Lord Glenbervie)*, 2 vols, 1928, vol. 2, p. 83.

Flora Fraser, *The Unruly Queen*, 1996.

Nathaniel Hawthorne, *Our Old Home*, 1863.

ARCADIAN LIFE AMONG THE COCKNEYS

Ronald Longhurst, 'Greenwich Fair', *Transactions of the Greenwich and Lewisham Antiquarian Society*, vol. 7, pp. 198–210.

Percival Leigh, *Mr Pips hys Diary*, 1849.

Charles Dickens in the *Evening Chronicle*, 1835.

Nathaniel Hawthorne, op. cit.

Robert Halliday, 'Beastly Business', *Country Life,* 9 December 1993.

Neil Rhind, op. cit.

The Pictorial Guide to Greenwich. A Holiday Handbook, 1884.

William Howarth, *Some Particulars Relating to the Ancient and Royal Borough of Greenwich*, 1882.

Cruikshank's Trip to Greenwich Fair, a Whimsical Record, 1830.

ALL HONOUR TO THE ENDERBYS

Mrs Thomas Norledge, 'Greenwich as an Ancient Fishing Port', *Transactions of the Greenwich and Lewisham Antiquarian Society*, vol. 1, 1915, pp. 356–72.

Philip Banbury, *Shipbuilders of the Thames and Medway*, Newton Abbot, 1971.

Alan Pearsall, 'Greenwich and the River in the 19th Century', *Transactions of the Greenwich and Lewisham Antiquarian Society*, vol. 8, 1973–8, pp. 20-26.

V. Bartlett, 'The River and Marsh at East Greenwich', *Transactions of the Greenwich and Lewisham Antiquarian Society*, vol. 7, 1964–72, pp. 68–85.

S. Shoberl, *A Summer's Day at Greenwich*, 1840.

R. H. G. Thomas, *London's First Railway: the London and Greenwich*, 1972.

June Burkitt, 'The Town of Greenwich in 1848', *Transactions of the Greenwich and Lewisham Antiquarian Society*, vol. 9, pp. 7–20.

Alec Holden, 'Early Town-planning in Greenwich', *Transactions of the Greenwich and Lewisham Antiquarian Society*, vol. 7, 1966, pp. 106–15.

The story of the *Cutty Sark* is told in the excellent Pitkin's guide, first published 1994.

THE WORLD SETS ITS WATCH

Illustrated London News, 14 May 1842, p. 16.

Derek Howse, *Greenwich Time*, op. cit.

PARASOL ON THE SUNNY STRAND OF THE FUTURE

Kevin Littlewood and Beverley Butler, *Of Ships and Stars, Maritime Heritage and the Founding of the National Maritime Museum*, Greenwich, 1998.

ILLUSTRATION SOURCES AND CREDITS

INDEX

Page numbers in *italics* refer to illustrations.

Adventure Gallery, 123
Airy, Sir George, 210-11, *218,* 219-20
Alberti, Leon Battista, 74
Alfege, St, 17, 19, 24-8
Allix, Dr, 152
Andrew, St, 25
Angerstein, John Julius, 16, 158-9, 161, 167, 169
Angerstein family, 159
Anne of Denmark, Queen, 22, 61, 63, 64-6, 67, 71-3, 75, 76, 77, 90, 129
Aretinus (i.e. Leonardo Bruni), 35
Ariel, 206
Armada, 56
Arnold, John, 218
Assemblée Nationale, 9
Assiter's Yard, 168, 175
Astronomers Royal, 9
Aubrey, John: *Brief Lives,* 104
Augusta, Princess, 160
Austin, Willie, 164

Babbage, Charles, 210
Babington, Uriah, 91
Bagwell, William, 99
Bankside Power Station, 170
Barber's Court, 168, 175
Barclay the Scot, 67

barges, 46
Basevi, George, 175
Basing House, Hampshire, 88
Bath, 25
Beattie, Dr, 166
Belvedere, The (Crooms Hill), 101
Belville, Ruth, 218
Benbow, Admiral John, 102
Bermondsey, 208
Bernini, Gian Lorenzo, 86-7
Bethell's Timber-Preserving Works, 205
Birmingham Philosophical Institution, 217
Blackheath, 10, 16, 34, 39, 94, 101, 156-7, 167, 180
    fashionable, 155
    Georgian amusements, 155, 176-8
    insurrections, (plate section 1) *2-3*
    lawlessness, 55, *40-41*
    royal connections, 85, 155
    soldiers on, 39-40, 43, 52, 90
    and Vikings, 24
Blackheath Avenue, 98
Blackheath Caverns, 177-8
Blackheath Golf Club, 11, 177
Blackheath Hill, 167
Blackheath Park, 160, 164, 171, 185
Blackheath Rangers, 164, 176
Blackheath Volunteer Cavalry, 176

242

Blackwall Tunnel, 224, 227
Blakely Ordnance Works, 205
Blenheim, man of war, 179
Blenheim Palace, 142-3
Blount, Thomas, 94, 101, 169
Blue Coat School, 12
    see also Christ's Hospital
Boleyn, Anne, 46, 53
Boreman, Sir William, 153
Bow Creek, 199
Bowles, William Lisle, 118
Bridge Street, 212
Brighton Pavillion, 161
*Britannia Sancta, or the Lives of
    the Most Celebrated British,
    English, Scottish and Irish Saints*,
    24
Britannia, whaler, 198
British Telecom, 15
Brunel, Isambard Kingdom, 199
Brunswick, Duke of, 160
Buccleuch, Duchess of, 160
Buchanan, George, 63
Buckingham, George Villiers,
    Duke of, 70, 77, 79, 81, 86,
    143
Buckingham Palace, 161
Bugg's Pond, 168
Bull, William, 224-5
Burke, Edmund, 178
Burns, Robert: 'Tam O'Shanter',
    188
Burton, Robert: *The Anatomy of
    Melancholy*, 67

Cade, Jack, 10, 16, 39
Cade Road, 39
Campbell, Colen, 130
    Vitruvius Britannicus, 82
Campe, Joachim Heinrich, 163

Canaletto (i.e. Giovanni Antonio
    Canal), 127
    View of Greenwich Park,
        (plate section 2) *4-5*
Canary Wharf, 14
Canterbury: Viking seige, 25-7
Canterbury Cathedral, (plate
    section 1) *1*
Capgrave, John: *Chronicles of
    England*, 36
Carew, Lord George, 66
Carleton, Lord Dudley, 65, 70-1
Carlisle, Lord, 141
Carlton House, 161
Caroline of Brunswick, Princess,
    134, 159, (plate section 2) *3*,
    160-4, 167, 187
Carpenters' Company, 131
Castle Hill, 180, 184
Castle Howard, Yorkshire, 141-3
Catherine of Aragon, 46, 47-8, 53
Cator, John, 169-70
Cecil, Robert, 61, 153
Ceylon Wharf, 202
Chamberlain, John, 65-6, 71, 74,
    166
Chapel Royal, 59
Chapman, Edmund, 153
Charles I, King, 70, 77-81, 85-8, 94
    art collection, 70-1, 91
    character, 78
    and Civil War, 87-8
    death, 88
    depicted, 77, 86
    and Inigo Jones, 77, 86, 88
    marriage, 79
Charles II, King, 81, 89, 91, 98,
    106, 126, 153
    establishes Royal
        Observatory, 106

interest in science, 107
his park, 97
his plans for Greenwich, 95-7, 98
and Seamen's Hospital, 121-2
visits Evelyn, 101
Charles V, Emperor, 49
Charlotte, Queen (formerly Princess), 85, 160, 163
Charlton, 21, 159
Charlton Fair, 150
Charterhouse, City of London, 62
Chatham Chest, 122
Chaucer, Geoffrey, 34, 144
Cheere, Sir Henry: Bust of Nicholas Hawksmoor, *29*
Chelsea Hospital, 122
Chesterfield, 5th Earl of, 158
Chesterfield House, 158, 160, 164
Chesterfield, Sir John Stanhope, 156-8, 160
Chesterfield, Philip Stanhope, 4th Earl of, 144,
Chesterfield Walk, 154
Chocolate House, Blackheath, 214
Christian IV, King of Denmark, 72
Christ's Hospital, Newgate Street, 114
    see also Blue Coat School
Church Street, 212
City of London, 10, 56, 62, 103, 154, 168, 204
Civil War, 87-8, 89-90, 94, 109, 143, 151
Clarence Street, 175
Claudius, Emperor, 21
Clement, Gregory, 94, 151
Clements, Captain John, 124
Cocke, Captain, 100

Cogan, Sir Andrew, 94, 100, 151
College Approach, 175
College Tunnel, 211
Collingwood, Admiral Cuthbert, 165
Colvin, Howard: *Biographical Dictionary of British Architects*, 159
Combe Farm, *213*
Comey family, 59
Commissioners for Longitude, 217
Contarini, Pietro, 75
Correr, Anzolo, 85, 86
Cottle, Mark, 100, 154
Court of Sewers, 202
Cranmer, Archbishop Thomas, 46
Creek Bridge, 185
Cromwell, Oliver, 91
Crooms Hill, 144, 152-4, 168
Crow, Captain M., 188-9
Crowley House, 13, *92-3*, 151
Crowley, Sir Ambrose, 13, 151
Crystal Palace, 219
Cutty Sark, 13, 188-9, 191, 227, 229

Daily Journal, 182
Davies, Michael, 226
Dayrolles, Solomon, 157
de Tocqueville, Alexis, 227
Defoe, Daniel, 129, 175
    Tour Through England and Wales, 151, 152
Delaporte, Gille, 33, 75
'Delicate Investigation', 162, 164
Denham, Sir John, 96
Denmark House, 66, 89
Deptford, 13, 56-7, 101, 102, 195, 208
    dockyard, 10, 52, 99, 164, 198

Derwentwater, Lord, 124, 132
DesBarre, J. F. W.: 'Atlantic
    Neptune', 221
Dickens, Charles, 182, 185, 186
    Our Mutual Friend, 190
Docklands Light Railway, 232
Dorset, Marquis of, 45
Douglas, Rev. James, 23
Dover Mail, 208
Dover Road, 145
Downes, Kerry, 140
Drake, Sir Francis, 12, 56
Draper, Sir William, 124, 129
Drummond, Lady, 67
Duke Humphrey's Tower, 35, 75,
    97, 109
    Giant's Steps, 97, 180, 232
    known as Greenwich Castle,
        110
    renamed Mireflore, 48
Dunstan, St, 25
Durkin, Richard, 86
Dutch House, Kew, 143
Dutch Wars, 91, 102

East Greenwich, 198, 203, 205,
    224
East Greenwich Madrigal Society,
    212
East India Company, 169, 198
Eastcheap North, City of London,
    154
Edgar, King, 23
Edinburgh, Prince Philip, Duke of,
    229
Edward III, King, 33
Edward IV, King (formerly Duke
    of York), 40-3
Edward, VI, King, 43, 54-5
Electric Telegraph Company, 220

Elizabeth I, Queen, 55-60, 61, 63-
    4, 91, 153
    appearance, 57
    armoury, 57, 63
    born at Greenwich Palace,
        12, 44
    court entertainments, 56-7,
        59, (plate section 1) 5
    and maritime developments,
        56
    meets Lambarde, 60
Elizabeth II, Queen, 230
Elizabeth of York, 42, 45
Elliot, Sir Gilbert *see* Minto, Lord
Elston (Observant Friar), 55
Enderby's Wharf, 202, 203
Equiano, Olaudah, 14
Ethelred, King, 27-8
Evelyn, John, 94-5, 119, 125, 143,
    155
    as connoisseur, 91
    first Treasurer of Seamen's
        Hospital, 121-122, 127,
        129
    Fumifugiom, 109
    as gardener, 102
    his ideas for Greenwich
        Palace, 96
    robbed, 94, 101
    visits Blackheath, 176
Evening Chronicle, 182
Execution Dock, 16, 202

*Fairburn's Edition of the Funeral of
    Admiral Lord Nelson*, 164-5
Fairfax, Thomas, 90
Fairy, 206
Fell, Bishop John, 114
Ferrabosco family, 59
Festival of Britain, 229, 230

Fish Offices, 91

Fitzherbert, Mrs Maria, 160

Flamsteed, John, 11, 107-8, 110, 111, 114-5, 122, (plate section 2) *1*
Historia Coelestis, 115

Flamsteed House, 230

Fleming, Sanford, 221

Ford motor company, 12

Fox, Sir Stephen, 121

Frederick, Prince of Wales, 124

Free Grammar School, 12

Friars Road, 175

Fubb's Yacht, 168

Fuseli, Henry, 159

Garter ceremonies, 70

Gazeteer, The, 182

Gentileschi, Orazio, 86

Gentleman's Magazine, 157, 179

George I, King, 85

George II, King, 123-4

George III, King, 10, 15, 160, 164

George IV, King (formerly Prince of Wales), 15, 158

Ghent, 144, 153

Gibson, George, 159

Gibson, Thomas, 107,
Portrait of John Flamsteed, (plate section 2) *1*

Gladstone, William, 187

Glenbervie, Lord, 161

Gloucester Circus, 168-9, 170, 180, 208, 227

Gloucester, Humphrey Duke of, 34-5, *37*, 38-9, 41
library, 35-6

Glover, Richard: 'Admiral Hosier's Ghost', 156

Golden Hind, 12-3, 56

Goldsmiths' Company, 94

Goose-pie House, Whitehall, 140-141, 142, 148

Gordon, Major, 167

Gothic Revival, 143, 148

Graham's Passage, 168

Grange, the (Cooms Hill), 153-4

Grant, Sir Archibald, 152

Great Bark, 52

Great Breach, 202

Great Eastern, 199, 204

Great Exhibition (1851), 219

Great Fire of London, 109

Great Gallery, 52

Great Harry, 52

Great Plague, 99, 102-4, 126

Great Western Railway, 219

Green Coat School, 12

Green Man tavern, 167, 208

Green, Valentine: *A Review of the Polite Arts in France*, 133

Greenwich Borough Museum, 21

Greenwich Fair, 14, 182-6, 230

Greenwich Hill, *181*, 180, 182

Greenwich Hospital *see* Royal Naval Hospital; Seamen's Hospital, Greenwich

Greenwich Improvement Act (1831), 175

Greenwich Inland Linoleum Company, 205

Greenwich Market, 94

Greenwich Marsh, *213*, 215, 225

Greenwich Mean Time, 9, 220-3

Greenwich Palace, 12, 46, 64, 89, 127
garden, 70
rebuilt by Charles II, 96-8
see also Placentia; Pleasaunce, manor of

Greenwich Park, 10, 14, 17, 22, 66, 80, 90, 94, 103, 139, 167, 168, 175, 179, 231
   amusements, 10, 14-5, 185
   depicted, (plate section 1) 6-7, 77, 134-5, (plate section 2) 4-5
   and railways, 187, 210
   Roman temple, 22
   Saxon barrows, 23
   as site for Royal Observatory, 109-10, 111, 180
   trees planted, 153
   waste ground, 91
Greenwich Railway, 182, 207-11, 216
Greenwich Society for the Diffusion of Useful Knowledge, 212
Grey Coat School, 12
Grey, Lady Jane, 55
Griffin, Thomas, 91
Grocers' Company, 153

Hall, Captain Basil, 217
Hall, Edward, 51
Halley, Edmond, 115
Hamilton, Briton, 13
Hamilton, Emma, 167
Hampton Court, Middlesex, 50
Hanmer, Sir Thomas: Garden Book, 95
Hardy, Sir Thomas, 133, 210
Hasted, Edward: History of Kent, 15, 178-9
Hawkins, Sir John, 56
Hawksmoor, Nicholas, 17, 29, 29, 85, 99, 125-8, 132, 154, 227
Hawthorne, Nathaniel: Our Old Home, 171, 174, 179, 185-6

Hayman, Miss (Princess Caroline's steward), 161
Heath Gate House, 153
Henham, Richard, 39
Henri IV, King of France, 79
Henrietta Anne, Duchess of Orleans, 89, 106
Henrietta Maria, Queen Consort, 77, 79-81, 85-88, 89-90, 95, 96-97, 101
Henry III, King, 10
Henry, Prince of Wales, 74
Henry V, King, 33, 34, 39
Henry VI, King, 34, 36, 42
Henry VII, King, 42, 43-5
Henry VIII, King, 12, 14, 17, 44, 45-54, 57, (plate section 1) 4, 67, 72, 126, 199
Hentzner, Paul, 56, 57-9
Herstmonceux Castle, Sussex, 230
Hewes, Richard, 90
highwaymen, 179-80
Hill, Sir Rowland, 217
Hillier, N., 152
Hilton (showman), 184
Hipparchus, 221
Hofland, Thomas,
Hogarth, William: Portrait of Inigo Jones, (plate section 1) 8
Hooke, Robert, 110, 114-5, 154
Hooker, Alderman, 154
Hooker, Sir William, 153
Hopton, John, 52
Horse Shoe Breach, 202
Hosier, Admiral Francis, 155-6
How, J., 134-5, 136
Howard, Henry, Earl of Northampton, 66-7
Howard, Thomas, Earl of Arundel, 66-7, 73

Howarth, W.: *Greenwich Past and Present*, 214
Hudson River Tunnel, 224
Hundred Years War, 33
Huntingdon, Lord, 139-40
Hutchinson, Mrs (Puritan critic), 78
Hyde Park, 108

Illustrated London News, 185, 217
Implacable, HMS, 229
Improved Wood Pavement Company, 205
International Geographical Congress (1871), 221
International Meridian Conference (1874), 221
Invalides, Les, Paris, 121, 132-3
Isle of Dogs, 22, 224, *228*

Jack of the Green, 179
James I, King of England (VI of Scotland), 61-6, 70-4, 75, 76, 97, 109, 177
    Counterblaste to Tobacco, 64
James II, King (formerly Duke of York), 118-20
    and Seamen's Hospital, 119-20
James, John, 128-9, 154, 169
James, Thomas, 86
Jennings, Admiral Sir John, 123
Jersey, Lady, 134
John Bull, 210
John Ellis, fishing smack, 189
John Penn & Company, 199, *200-1*
Johnson, Samuel, 170
Joint-Services College, 138
Jones, Inigo, (plate section 1) *8*, 71-2, 73-4, 76, 77-8, 84, 86, 88, 96, 98, 229

Jonson, Ben, 71, 76
    Pan's Anniversary, or the Shepherds' Holiday, 72, 75
jousting, 50-51, *51*
Jubilee Line, 232

Kay, Joseph, 175, 191
Kellet, Mr (Blackheath resident), 152
Kent Road, 103
Kentish Mercury, 191
Kentish Railway Company, 206-7
Keroualle, Louise de, Duchess of Portsmouth, 106-7
Kidd, Captain William, 123
Kimbolton Castle, near Huntingdon, 142-3
King William Street, 175
King's College Chapel, Cambridge, 43
King's Head tavern, 103
Kit-Cat Club, 148
Kneller, Sir Godfrey, 102

la Roche, Sophie von, 136
Lake, Sir Lancelot, 153
Lake, Sir Thomas, 153
Lambarde, John, 60
Lambarde, William: *Account of the Records of the Tower*, 60, 145, 202, 210
Lambarde Wall, 202
Landmann, George, 207
Lanier family, 59, 153
Laniere, Jerome, 91
Latimer, Hugh, 43
Lawrence, Sir Thomas, 161, 162
    Portrait of Princess Caroline of Brunswick, (plate section 2) *3*

Le Nôtre, André, 97, 98
Leach's Alley, 168
Leland, John, 52
Lely, Sir Peter, 103
Less Bark, 52
Lewisham, 70, 220
Lewisham, manor of, 23
Literary Institute, 212
Lloyd's Coffee House, 158
Lloyd's of London, 158
Loampit Hill, Lewisham, 159
Lock, Mrs (visitor to Woodlands), 167
Lombard Wall, 102
Londinium, 21
London Bridge, 187, 194
London County Council, 227
London George, 102
London Scots Society, 177
London Seed Crushing Company, 205
longitude, calculation of, 9, 106-7, 221-2
Longueville, Duke of, 49
Louis XII, King of France, 48
Louis XIV, King of France, 89, 97, 106, 120, 121
Lumley, Baron, 60
Lysons, Samuel, 159

McBride, Captain, 189
Macartney House, 155
Machyn, Henry, 57
Maiden Row, 168
Manby, Captain Thomas, 162
Manchester, Lord, 143
Margaret of Anjou, 36, 38, 40
Margate, 119
Market Square, 168

Marlborough, John Churchill, 1st Duke of, 142
Marlborough, Sarah Jennings, Duchess of, 142
Mary I, Queen, 44, 49
Mary II, Queen, 119-20, 125-7, 155
Mary, Princess, 87
Mary Rose, 52
Mason, Robert, 143
masques, 72-3, 88, 178
Maudsley, Son & Field, 199, 215
Maze Hill, 139, 141, 142, 144-5, 148-9
Mell family, 59
Melville, Herman, 198
Melville, Thomas, 198
Mercury, The, 194
Millennium Dome, 10-7, (plate section 2) 8, 187, 198, 199, 202-3, 205, 229-30, 231-2
    Body zone, 16
    construction of, 226-7
    Faith zone, 17
    Home Planet zone, 13
    Journey zone, 12
    Learning zone, 15
    Living Island zone, 15
    Mind zone, 15
    Money zone, 14
    on New Year's Day 2000, 11
    Rest zone, 16
    Self-Portrait zone, 12
    Talk zone, 15
    Shared Ground zone, 13-4
    Work zone, 14-5
Milliennium Experience Company, 11, 226
Ministry of Defence, 231
Minto, Lord (Sir Gilbert Elliot), 162

Mitre tavern, 212
Molin, Nicolo, 65
Monconseil, Marquise de, 157
Montague, Lady Mary Wortley, 144
Montague, Lord, 14
Montague House, 14, 160, 162, 167
Moore, Sir Jonas, 104-5, *105*, 106, 107, 111
    A Mapp or Description of the River Thames, 104, 110
Morden, Sir John, 169
Morden College, 169
Mould Strand Wharf, 170
Museum of London, 20
Mycenae Road, 158

Naiad, paddle-steamer, 206
Napoleon III, Emperor, 162, 188
National Company for Boat Building by Machinery, 199, 215
National Gallery, 16, 158, 230
National Gallery of Naval Art, 230
National Lottery, 230
National Maritime Museum, 15, 78, 138, 167, 229, 230
    Neptune Court, 231
Nautical Almanac, 221
Navigation Act (1651), 91
Navy Board, 121, 126
Nelson Street, 175
Nelson, Viscount Horacio, 16, 133, 164-7, 210
    funeral, 16, (plate section 2) *2*, 164-6, 170, 229
New Kent Road, 170
Newcastle, Duke of, 145
Newell, Philip, 137-8

Newmarket Palace, 74
Newton, Sir Isaac, 11, 111, 115
Nicholas of the Tower, 39
Nixon, Samuel, 175
Norfolk College (Trinity Hospital), *68-9*
Norledge, Mrs Thomas, 188, 189
Northumberland, Duke of (Lord Protector), 54, 55
Norwich, Earl of, 90
Noviomagus, 22
Nymph, 206

Oatlands Palace, Surrey, 66
Observant Friars, 17, 42
Office of Works, 55
Old Court, 187
Old Ford, 222
One Tree Hill, Greenwich park, (plate section 2) *6-7*
Orleans, Duke of, 89
Osboldston, Robert, 123, 154
Osler, Abraham Follett, 217
Oxford University, 36

paddle-steamers, 206
Page, Sir Gregory, 169, 176
Page, Jenny, 11, 226
Pagoda, Montague House, 161, 163
Pagoda Road, Blackheath, 161
Palladio, Andrea, 73-4, 76
Paragon, Blackheath, 169-71, *172-3*, 180, 208, 227
Paris Mean Time, 9, 222-3
Park Hall, Crooms Hill, 154
Paternoster Croft, 153
Pearson, Sir Weetman, 224
Pegge, Samuel, 109

Pelican, see Golden Hind
Pennington, Mrs (friend of Pepys), 103
Pennant, Thomas, 152
Penny Magazine, 209
People, The, 195
Pepys, Samuel, 14, 99-101, 118-9, 178
    character, 99, 103
    on Charles II park, 97, 99
    escapes the Plague, 102-3
    on James II, 119
    and Jonas Moore, 104, 106
    at the Navy Board, 121, 155
    and the Seamen's Hospital, 121, 124-6
    visits dockyards, 99
    visits friends in Greenwich, 94-5, 99-100, 102-3, 154
Peter the Great, 102
Peter Pomegranate, 52
Peto, William (Observant Friar), 17, 53, 55
Philip II, King of Spain, 55
Phoenix Gas Company, 212
Pilot public house, 202
Place, Francis, 111, 114, 154
Placentia, 12, 14, 43, 44-5, 54, 55, 59-60, 66, 94, 95, 126, 199
    see also Greenwich Palace; Plesaunce, manor of
plague, 67
    see also Great Plague
Plesaunce, manor of, 35
    see also Placentia
Polytechnic of East London, 138
Pomphret, Lord, 152
Pond, John, 38, 216
Pope, Alexander, 131, 156
Port of London, 189

Porter, Endymion, 77
Portsmouth, 52, 119
    Harbour, 216
Post Office, 217, 219
prime meridian, 221-2
Prince (flagship), 118
Princes in the Tower, 42
Procession Oak, outside Bromley, 94
Pruddle, John, 38
Public Record Office, 60

Quarterly Review, 206
Queen Elizabeth's College, 12, 60
Queen's House, 77-8, *82-83*, 89, 91, 98, 126-7, 132, 168, 229, 230
    begun by Anne of Denmark, 64, 71, 73
    building recommences, 79, 81
    chimneypieces, 86
    classical design, 76
    completed for Henrietta Maria, 86-7
    damaged, 96
    early design, 74-5, 81
    functions, 75-6, 85, 126
    modified, 81, 84, 86-7
    as a novelty, 74
    occupied by Royal Hospital School, 231
    paintings in, 86, 87
    proportions, 76
    and railways, 210
    reconstructed by Charles II, 96-7
    temporary roof, 81

Raleigh, Sir Walter, 57, 75

Ranger's House, Blackheath, 155, 158

Regent, The, 52

Rennie, Sir John, 210

Rhind, Neil: *The Heath*, 176

Richard II, King, 60

Richard III, King, 42

Richard Rogers Associates, 226

Richardson, Henry H., 175

Richardson's Theatre, 185

Richelieu, Cardinal Armand Duplessis, Duc de, 79

Richmond, 2nd Duke of, 155

Richmond Palace (formerly Sheen), 44

Richmond, Surrey, 156

Ripley, Thomas, 131-2

Robinson, Henry, 39

Rocque, John: *Survey of London*, 21, *26*

Rolls Chapel, 60

Romans, 20-1

Romney, Lord, 123

Romney Road, 168

Round Tower, Montague House, 160-1

Royal Albert Dock, 204

Royal Alfred Aged Merchant Seamen's Institution, 191

Royal Dock, 204

Royal James, 100

Royal Naval College, 15, 98, 138, 231

Royal Naval Hospital, 11, 12, 15, 16, 99, 170, 187
    see also Royal Naval College; Seamen's Hospital, Greenwich; University of Greenwich

Royal Naval Museum, 230

Royal Navy, 123, 216, 231

Royal Observatory, 9 15, 35, 106, 108-110, 114-5, *116-7*, 121, 180, 182, 187, 210, 215-6, 218
    future plans, 109
    and Herstmonceux, 230
    Octagon Room, *112-3*, 230
    time signals, 219-20
    timeball, 114

Royal Society, 15, 101, 107, 109, 121, 124, 176, 227

Royston, Hertfordshire, 62

Ruskin, John, 142
    Fors Clavigera, 184

Russell, Edmond, 28

Russell, P.: *England Displayed*, 178

Ruyter, Michiel de, 118

Ryder, Richard, 153

Rysbrack, John, 123

St Albans, Earl of, 96

St Alfege's, parish church, 19, *30-31*, 128, 154, 155, 158, 189, 212
    bombed in Second World War, 227
    rebuilt, 28-9, 150

St James's Palace, 81, 106, 132

St Mary's Church, 175, 214

St Michael (flagship), 118

St Paul's Cathedral, 109, 128, 129
    Lord Nelson's funeral, 165

St Paul's Church, Covent Garden, 81

St Peter's Abbey, Ghent, 23, 32, 33

St Pierre, Le Sieur de, 107

St Thomas's Hospital, 121

Salmon, Richard, 91

Samuel Enderby & Sons, 198

Sancho, Ignatius, 14
  Letters, 14
Sandwich, Edward Montagu, 1st
  Earl of, 119
Saunders (showman), 184
Saye and Sele, Lord, 39
Sayes Court, Deptford, 101-2, 121
Scamozzi, Vincenzo, 74
Scaramelli, Giovanni Carlo, 63
Science Museum, 230
Scott, Sir Walter: *Kenilworth*, 57
Seamen's Hospital, Greenwich, 67,
  87, 109, 115, 119-38, 139, 154,
  164-6, 167, 168, 175, 208, 212,
  229-31
    Chapel, 138
    Great Hall, 128, 129
    history of, 119-124
    infirmary, 175
    King Charles Court, 124,
      134
    King Charles Wing, 98, 126-
      9
    Painted Hall, 130, 138, 154,
      164, 166, 229-30
    Pensioners, 134-8, 166, 184
    Pensioners' uniforms, 137
    Record Room, 164
Searles, Michael, 168-9
Second World War, 227, 229
Shakespeare, William, 64
    Macbeth, 64
    *A Midsummer Night's
      Dream*, 59
Sherburn, Sir Edward, 70
Shilibeer, George, 208-9
Ship tavern, 17, 153, 190-1, 227
Shooters Hill, 21
Shovell, Admiral Sir Cloudesley,
  151

Signoret, Mr (merchant), 152
Sleaman, J., 178
Sloane, Sir Hans, 176
Smith, Sir Sidney, 162
Smith, William, 153
Snape, Andrew, 154-5
Somerset House, 89
Sophia (daughter of James I), 65
South Eastern Railway, 220
South Foreland, 123
South Metropolitan Gas Company,
  205
South Sea Bubble, 207
Southey, Robert: *Letters from
  England*, 132
Southwold Bay, Battle of, 118-9
Sovereign of the Seas, 86
Spinelli, Gasparo, 50
Stagg Court, 175
standard time, 217, 219-23
Stocks Lane, 168
Stranger's Guide to Greenwich
  (1855), 214
Stuart, James 'Athenian', 128, 229
Suffolk, Countess of, 156
Suffolk, Duke of, 38-9
'Swanne House', 94
Sweyn (Danish leader), 27
Swift, Jonathan, 140
Sylph, 206

Tailer, Zachary, 87
Tallis, Thomas, 59
Talman, William, 141
Tavern Row, 175
Taylor, Sir Robert, 159
Taylor's Rents, 175
Thames Conservancy, 195
Thames Ironworks & Shipbuilding
  Company, 199

Thames River, 19-21, 164-6, 194, 198, 224-5
    frozen, 101
    Roman settlements, 20-1
    survey, 104
    wildlife, 19-20
Theobalds, Hertfordshire, 61, 62, 65
Thornhill, Sir James, 129-30, 133
Thrale, Mrs Hester, 170
Thunderer, battleship, 199
Thurkill (commander of the Danes), 27
Tilbury, 111
Timbs, John: *Club Life of London*, 191
Times, The, 170-1, 184
Tom Tower, Oxford, 110
Tompion, Thomas, 114
Tonson, Jacob, 148
Tower Bridge, 224
Tower of London, 62
Townley, Mr (inventor), 108, 114
Trafalgar, Battle of, 16, 164, 166, 167
Trafalgar tavern, 17, 190-1, 194
Trinity Hospital, 12, 67
Tudor, Mary, 48, 55
Turpin Lane, 188
Twickenham, Middlesex, 156
Tyler, Wat, 39
Tyrawley, Lord, 158

UNESCO World Heritage Site, 231
Universal Time, 9, 222-3
University of Greenwich, 15, 138, 231

Van Belcamp, Jan, 77, 81
Van Dyck, Sir Anthony, 71, 77, 87
Van Stalbemt, Adriaen, 77, 81
Vanbrugh, Charles, 148
Vanbrugh Jr, Charles, 148-9
Vanbrugh House, 139-42, 148
Vanbrugh Jr, John, 148-9
Vanbrugh, Philip, 148
Vanbrugh, Sir John, 125, 127, 130, 139-45, 148-9, 150, 152, 154
    The Provok'd Wife, 140
    The Relapse, 140
Vanbrugh, William, 129
Vanbrugh's Castle, 143-5, *146-7*, 148-9, 154, 158
Versailles, 97
Vertue, Robert, 45
Vickers, K. H., 35, 36
Victoria, Queen, 191
Victoria and Albert Museum, 230
Victory, HMS, 165-6
Voltaire, François Marie Aronet de, 182

Walpole, Horace, 148, 152
Walpole, Sir Robert, 131
Walter, George, 207
Wapping, 202
Ware, Isaac, 156-7
Wars of the Roses, 40
Wat Tyler Club, 214
Waterloo, Battle of, 206
Watling Street, 21-3
Wauchope, Captain Robert, 216
Webb, John, 88, 96, 98-9
    Historical Essay on the Origins of the Chinese Language, 98-9
Weddel, Mrs (visitor to Woodlands), 159

Westcombe Manor, 60, 145
Westminster Abbey, 55
whaling, 13, 194-5, *196-7*, 198
whitebait suppers, 190-1, *192-3*
Whitehall, 63, 106, 131, 165-6
  Palace, 55, 62, 81, 88, 89, 140
Whitlock, Bulstrode, 91
Wilbraham, Sir Roger, 61
William I, King, 'the Conqueror',
  47
William II, Prince of Orange, 87
William III, King, 102, 119-20,
  129, 155
William IV, King, 175
William Kuper & Company, 15,
  203
Wilson, George, 177
Wolfe, Major-General James, 98,
  155
Wollaston, William Hyde, 217
Wolsey, Cardinal Thomas, 49, 54
Wombell's Menagerie, 184-5
Woodlands home farm, *213*
Woodlands House, 16, 158, 159,
  167, 169
Woodstock manor, 142
Woodville, Elizabeth, 42

Woolwich, 86, 100, 103, 195
  dockyard, 10, 52, 99
Wootton, Sir Henry, 64
Worley, John, 133, 137
Wren Jr, Christopher: *Parentalia*,
  99, 125
Wren, Sir Christopher, 99, 124-30,
  231
    architect of Royal Naval
      Hospital, 99, 124-30, 168
    assistants, 29, 125-6, 128,
      129, 154
    chooses site for Royal
      Observatory, 109, 110-1
    inspects damage to Sayes
      Court, 102
    and Vanbrugh, 125, 127,
      139, 141, 144
Wren Society, 127
Wricklemarsh House, 94, 169,
  171, 176
Wyatt, Sir Thomas, 55
Wyngaerde, Anthony, 55

Yarborrough, Mrs (later Lady
  Vanbrugh), 144
York, Duke of, 44